The
Bean
Cookbook

The Bean Cookbook

Dry Legume Cookery

by Norma S. Upson

Pacific Search Press

Pacific Search Press, 222 Dexter Avenue North,
    Seattle, WA 98109
© 1982 by Norma S. Upson. All rights reserved
Printed in the United States of America

Designed by Judy Petry

Library of Congress Cataloging in Publication Data

Upson, Norma.
    The bean cookbook.

    Includes index.
    1. Cookery (Beans)   I. Title.
TX803.B4U67 1982   641.6'565   82-12487
ISBN 0-914718-72-X (pbk.)

A bean cookbook for Johnny Bright who asked for it

Contents

About Beans

Since the beginning of recorded history, dried beans and beanlike legumes have been the most crucial ingredient in the traditional diets of the world population. Archaeologists in Mexico have found evidence that as long ago as 7000 B.C. beans were used in the primary diets of our South-of-the-Border neighbors. Remains of lentils found in Egyptian tombs date back more than four thousand years, and wall paintings from 1200 B.C. illustrate the preparation of foods made from lentils. China and India always have given their highest regard to the bean family, and soybeans and mung beans have been the culinary delight of their royalty through the ages. In fact, everywhere in the world beans in one form or another—the "poor man's meat"—have been a nutritional mainstay and often the prime source of proteinaceous foods.

In Mexico kidney beans of all sizes are favored, while Cuba cherishes its black bean. In the New England states, navy beans, so called because they were an important and easily preserved protein food aboard ships, are favored along with cranberry beans and white beans; in the South and Southwest red beans, pinto beans, and black-eyed peas find their way into regional recipes. As new cultures are introduced into America, so also are new bean recipes.

Beans are about twenty to twenty-five percent protein, but they do not contain all of the essential amino acids and thus their protein is incomplete. However, complete protein can be formed by coupling beans with other protein sources. Grains, particularly rice, corn, and wheat, are an excellent partner for beans. Beans lack the essential amino acid methionine; grains are abundant in this amino acid. Grains are deficient, however, in another essential amino acid, lysine, whereas beans have a high lysine content. So the combination of grain and beans is a good source—and a very economical one—of high quality protein that the body can readily synthesize.

It is interesting to note that long before diet was consciously consid-ered, mankind turned to grain–bean combinations for protein. There seems to be a natural affinity between beans and corn, beans and rice, and, of course, beans and corn bread or brown bread. Experiments have shown that rice and black beans, a favorite dish in Cuba, Costa Rica, and other Latin American countries, is prepared with the correct proportion of rice to beans (eighty percent rice to twenty percent beans is the standard recipe) to produce a perfectly balanced protein dish. Corn bread and crowder peas (field peas), a traditional combination in the Southern states, are mixed in equal portions to produce the correct balance. And so it goes. In every case, bean dishes that have become tradi-tional throughout the world seem to be the result of an instinctive balan-cing of beans and complementary grains to produce complete protein.

Bean–grain combinations even have some nutritional advantages over meat. Experiments have shown that the bean-grain combinations lower blood fats and decrease hardening of the arteries. In diets con-ducted by nutritionists, serum cholesterol levels declined by nine per-cent when legumes and grains were used instead of meat as the primary source of protein. Indeed, beans have much to offer nutritionally. They are rich in iron, high in fiber content (which aids in digestion), and low in calories. And they also contain many vitamins and minerals that are essential to good health.

But despite the fact that beans are both inexpensive and healthful, many people will not eat them because they find them difficult to digest or because they cause intestinal gas. Intestinal gas that is associated with beans is caused primarily by two unusual starches, stachyose and raffinose. They are not easily broken down by digestive enzymes, so they remain in the digestive tract, where they come in contact with intestinal bacteria. This bacteria breaks the starches down into carbon dioxide and hydrogen, which are the main components of intestinal gas.

Incorporating some additional steps into the preparation of dried beans will eliminate this problem. Sort and wash the beans and cover them with water. Soak them all day, then before going to bed at night, put them in the freezer. Freezing beans overnight breaks down the starch molecules. Cook the beans without salt until they are almost tender, then add meat tenderizer containing papaya. Since the tender-izer contains salt, there is no need to add salt. (Six papaya tablets or two tablespoons of papaya granules, plus salt, may be used instead of the tenderizer.) Because this method is time consuming, you might want to prepare two to three times the amount of beans you need and freeze the excess for later use. Or, simpler still, just give your digestive system a chance to get used to beans by consuming them in small quantities at first and gradually increasing your intake. Your system will learn to ac-commodate them.

General Instructions for Cooking Dried Beans

The conventional method for cooking dried beans is as follows. Sort and wash the beans and cover them with water (a general guideline is to use three to four times as much water as beans), then let them soak overnight. (Or use the quick-soak method: boil the beans for two minutes, then cover the pot and let them stand for one hour.) Bring them to a boil, reduce heat, and simmer, partially covered, until the beans are tender. Add salt (about ¼ teaspoon per cup of beans) and use as directed in your recipe.

Cooking times vary widely according to the type of beans, where they were grown, how old they are, and many other factors. You just have to watch them and keep checking for tenderness. (A pressure cooker often can be used to shorten cooking time.) Soybeans, however, take longer to cook than any other beans. Their cooking time can be significantly reduced, though, by soaking them overnight and then freezing them in the soaking water. Allow them to thaw, then cook until they are tender. To test beans for tenderness, place a bean on your tongue and press it against the roof of your mouth. If it crushes easily, it is done; if not, reheat the beans and simmer until done.

Keep in mind that the beans will swell during the soaking and cooking processes, so they probably will measure about twice as much after cooking as they did dry. This is an important distinction in this cookbook because in some of the recipes the specified amount of beans should be measured after cooking. In these cases, the amount and the specification "cooked" are not separated by a comma (for example, *2 cups cooked*). If the beans are to be measured before cooking, the amount and any further specifications *are* separated by a comma (for example, *1 cup, cooked and mashed*). (If the beans on the ingredients list are not designated as "cooked," the beans should be measured in their dry form, then soaked, and then prepared as specifically directed in the recipe instructions.)

Appetizers

Yucatan Black Bean Dip

Black beans 1 pound
Water 6 cups
Salt 1 teaspoon
Lean ground pork 1 pound
Oregano 2 teaspoons
Butter 2 tablespoons
Onion 1 cup chopped
Medium radishes 5, sliced
Hot green chili peppers 1 to 4 teaspoons peeled,
   seeded, and chopped
Lemon juice 6 tablespoons
Salt 2 teaspoons
Green chili salsa 1 cup
Monterey Jack cheese 8 ounces, shredded
Fresh coriander leaves or parsley ¼ cup chopped
Taco chips

Soak beans overnight or quick-soak; drain. Combine beans, water, and 1 teaspoon salt and cook about 2 to 3 hours until beans are tender. Remove beans and set aside. Bring stock to a boil and add pork and oregano. Bring to a boil again, then drain and set aside pork. Melt butter in a large heavy skillet. Sauté onions, radishes, and peppers until limp. Add beans, cooked pork, lemon juice, and 2 teaspoons salt. Lower heat and simmer 10 to 15 minutes, stirring to prevent sticking. Add chili salsa and cheese and continue simmering until cheese melts. Pour dip into a serving dish, sprinkle with coriander, and surround with taco chips. Serve warm. Makes 2½ to 3 cups.

Middle Eastern Garbanzo Dip

Sesame seeds ¼ cup, toasted
Garbanzos 2 cups cooked, liquid drained and 1 tablespoon reserved
Salt ½ teaspoon
Lemon juice ¼ cup
Garlic powder 1½ teaspoons
Vegetable oil 1 tablespoon
Sesame oil ½ teaspoon
Tabasco sauce dash

In blender, grind sesame seeds to a fine consistency. Add garbanzos and reserved liquid and puree. Add remaining ingredients and blend well. Place in a bowl and allow to set at room temperature at least 1 hour to blend flavors. Serve as a dip for fresh vegetables, crackers, or pita bread. Makes about 1¼ cups.

Hummus

Garbanzos   2 cups cooked
Garlic cloves   1 or 2, minced
Tahini   2 tablespoons
Lemon juice   2 tablespoons or to taste
Olive oil   ½ teaspoon
Soy sauce   to taste
Salt   to taste
Parsley sprigs or mint leaves   garnish

Puree garbanzos and mix in remaining ingredients except parsley. Garnish and serve with crackers, flat bread, or pita pieces. Makes 2 cups.

Healthy Bean Dip

Pinto beans   4 cups cooked and mashed
Water   1 cup
Onions   1 cup chopped
Garlic clove   1, minced
Cumin seed   1 teaspoon
Jalapeño peppers   2, chopped
Large tomatoes   4, chopped
Molasses   1 tablespoon
Lemon juice   of 1 lemon
Chili powder   3 tablespoons
Salt   1½ teaspoons
Oil   ½ cup
Sharp Cheddar cheese   8 ounces, shredded

Put first 8 ingredients in a large kettle and simmer 1 hour. Add lemon juice, chili powder, and salt. While still hot, add oil and cheese. Mash and blend thoroughly. Serve hot or cold with chips or crackers. Makes 4 cups.

Ceci Marinara

Garbanzos 4 cups cooked, liquid drained and reserved, or
  Canned garbanzos two 16-ounce cans
Olive oil ½ cup
Anchovy fillets 2-ounce can, drained and finely chopped
Salt ½ teaspoon
Pepper 1 teaspoon
Parsley 3 tablespoons chopped

Slowly heat garbanzos in a small amount of their liquid. In another saucepan, heat oil and add remaining ingredients. Cook over low heat, stirring frequently. Pour over heated garbanzos, stir well, and cook about 15 minutes more until heated through. Chill in sauce at least 6 hours. Serves 6 to 8.

Garbanzo Nuts

Garbanzos 1 pound
Salt
Water
Butter ½ cup
Garlic cloves 4, crushed
Dry mustard ½ teaspoon
Chili powder 1 teaspoon
Salt 2 teaspoons
Onion salt 1 teaspoon
Ginger 1 teaspoon
Garlic salt ½ teaspoon
Soy sauce 1 tablespoon

Soak garbanzos overnight or quick-soak; drain. Cook garbanzos in well-salted water about 1 hour until nearly done but still a bit hard. Drain and divide into 2 equal portions. Melt ½ butter and sauté ½ garlic in each of 2 skillets. Remove the garlic and place ½ garbanzos in each pan. Sauté very slowly, turning and stirring often, until beans begin to sizzle and turn a dark golden brown. When crunchy on the outside and tender inside, they are done. Meanwhile, mix together mustard, chili powder, salt, and onion salt in a bowl and mix ginger, garlic salt, and soy sauce in another bowl. Sprinkle each mixture over ½ the garbanzos and toss lightly to coat. Serve hot in separate bowls. These can be made ahead and reheated in the oven at 350° for 2 to 5 minutes. Makes 2 to 3 cups.

Bombay Chiura

Lentils ¼ cup
Split peas ¼ cup
Long grain rice ¼ cup
Water 3 cups
Oil 2 tablespoons
Cayenne ⅛ teaspoon
Ground cloves ¼ teaspoon
Salt to taste
Ground coriander 1 teaspoon
Ground cumin 1 teaspoon
Turmeric ½ teaspoon
Sesame seeds 1 teaspoon
Salted peanuts ½ cup
Salted cashews ½ cup
Raisins ¼ cup

Rinse lentils, peas, and rice; place in a pan, add water, and bring to a boil. Boil 1 minute. Remove from heat, cover, and allow to set 15 minutes. Drain, rinse with cold water and drain again; then spread on paper towels and pat to dry. Heat oil in a frying pan over medium heat. Add lentils, peas, and rice and stir well. Add seasonings and sesame seeds and cook, stirring constantly, about 12 to 15 minutes, until mixture is lightly toasted. Remove from heat and add remaining ingredients. Cool and store in airtight container; keeps up to 10 days. Serve as cocktail snacks. Makes 2 cups.

Oven-Roasted Soybeans

Use the largest kind of soybeans available. Place beans in pot, cover with water, and soak for 24 hours. Bring to a boil, then simmer about 1½ hours until beans are just tender. Drain well. Spread beans in a shallow pan and roast at 350° about 30 minutes until brown, stirring occasionally to ensure even browning. Sprinkle with butter and salt or with garlic salt and soy sauce, if desired, to taste. Use in any way nuts might be used, such as in salads or cookies.

Salads

Any-Bean Vinaigrette

Flageolets, Great Northern beans, or any white bean   1½ cups
Water   2 quarts
Basil leaves   1 teaspoon
Ground thyme   ½ teaspoon
Pepper   ½ teaspoon
Bouquet garni*
Salt   3½ teaspoons
Olive oil   3 tablespoons
Lemon juice   3 tablespoons
Onion   ¼ cup finely chopped
Parsley   ¼ cup finely chopped

Soak beans overnight or quick-soak; drain. Put beans in saucepan with water and next 4 ingredients and cook until tender, adding salt when beans are almost tender. Drain thoroughly and chill several hours. Half an hour before serving combine remaining ingredients, reserving some of the parsley to sprinkle over salad; pour over beans and toss. Return to refrigerator until serving time. Garnish with remaining parsley and serve as a first course. Serves 8.
* Bay leaf, celery tops, parsley sprigs, and garlic cloves tied in a cheese-cloth bag.

Black-eyed Pea and Rice Salad

Long grain rice   2 cups cooked
Black-eyed peas   2 cups cooked, drained, and rinsed, or
    Canned black-eyed peas   16-ounce can, drained
Green onions   ½ cup thinly sliced
Celery   ½ cup chopped
Parsley   ¼ cup chopped
Pimiento   2 tablespoons chopped
Olive oil   ¼ cup
Red wine vinegar   ¼ cup
Worcestershire sauce   1 teaspoon
Salt   ½ teaspoon
Orange peel   ½ teaspoon grated
Tabasco sauce   ¼ teaspoon
Lettuce
Orange slices   garnish
Ripe olives   garnish

Combine rice and peas; add onions, celery, parsley, and pimiento and mix well. Stir together next 6 ingredients and pour over bean mixture. Cover and chill 1 to 24 hours. Serve on lettuce with garnish of orange slices and olives. Serves 6 to 8.

Garbanzo–Green Bean Salad

Garbanzos   2 cups cooked or
    Canned garbanzos   15-ounce can, drained
Frozen French-cut green beans   two 10-ounce packages,
    thawed and drained
Celery   1 cup thinly sliced
Garlic clove   1, finely minced
Wine vinegar   ¼ cup
Salad oil   ¼ cup
Sugar   1 tablespoon
Salt   ½ teaspoon
Basil   ½ teaspoon crushed
Lettuce

Combine first 4 ingredients in a bowl. Combine remaining ingredients except lettuce and pour over the beans, mixing well to coat each bean. Refrigerate 4 to 6 hours. To serve, mix gently and place in a lettuce-lined shallow bowl. Serves 6 to 8.

Italian Mixed Green Salad

Lettuce or salad greens 1 quart torn into pieces
Medium tomatoes 2, peeled and cut into wedges
Small zucchini 1, thinly sliced
Garbanzos 1 cup cooked or
   Canned garbanzos 8¾-ounce can, drained
Monterey Jack cheese 5 ounces, cubed
Dry salami or pepperoni 2 ounces, very thinly sliced
Croutons ½ cup
Salt and pepper to taste
Italian dressing

Wash and drain lettuce, chill until crisp, and place in a bowl. Add next 6 ingredients, sprinkle with salt and pepper, and toss lightly with dressing. Serves 4 to 8.

Italian Supper Salad

Romaine or mixed greens 1 quart chilled and torn into pieces
Medium tomatoes 2, peeled and cut into wedges
Small zucchini 1, sliced
Garbanzos 2 cups cooked
Monterey Jack cheese 6 ounces, cubed
Dry salami 2 ounces, skinned and sliced paper-thin
Croutons ½ cup
Salt and pepper to taste
Italian dressing

In a salad bowl, toss together first 5 ingredients. Cover with salami slices and croutons, season with salt and pepper, and top with Italian dressing. Serves 4 to 6.

Salad Burritos

Garbanzos or kidney beans 1 cup cooked
Pitted ripe olives ½ cup sliced
Onion ½, thinly sliced and separated into rings
Oil ½ cup
Vinegar 3 tablespoons
Taco seasoning mix half 1¼-ounce package
Sugar ½ teaspoon
Monterey Jack cheese 8 ounces, shredded
Lettuce 1 head, shredded
Small bell pepper 1, seeded and chopped
Flour tortillas 12, fried
Salsa topping
Shredded cheese garnish

Combine beans, olives, and onion in a bowl. Mix together next 4 ingredients, pour over bean mixture, and chill. Add cheese, lettuce, and pepper to chilled beans and toss. Spoon ½ cup of the mixture on each warm tortilla and serve with salsa and additional cheese if desired. Serves 12.

Meat and Bean Salad

Large garlic clove 1, minced
Salt 1 teaspoon
Basil ½ teaspoon
Pepper ½ teaspoon
Red wine vinegar ⅓ cup
Red kidney beans 2 cups cooked or
    Canned red kidney beans 16-ounce can, drained
Cut green beans 16-ounce can, drained
Garbanzos 1½ cups cooked or
    Canned garbanzos 1½ cups drained
Salami or pepperoni 1½ cups (6 ounces) julienne-cut
Large tomato 1, seeded and chopped
Onion 1 cup chopped
Canned green chili peppers 2 tablespoons chopped
Salad greens

Combine first 5 ingredients in a large bowl and blend well. Add remaining ingredients except greens and toss to mix. Refrigerate 6 hours or overnight to blend flavors. Serve on greens. Serves 4 to 6.

Rancho Salad

Kidney beans   2½ to 3 cups cooked or
   Canned kidney beans   2½ to 3 cups drained
White beans   2½ to 3 cups cooked or
   Canned cannellini beans   2½ to 3 cups drained
Garbanzos   2 cups, cooked, or
   Canned garbanzos   two 16-ounce cans, drained
Large onion   1, coarsely chopped, or
   Green onions   12, chopped
Pimientos   3, chopped
Celery   3 stalks, chopped
Stuffed green olives   12 to 18, sliced
Green peppers   2, seeded and chopped
Fresh parsley   ½ to 1 cup chopped or to taste
Olive oil   ⅓ cup
Wine vinegar   3 to 4 tablespoons
Garlic cloves   2, crushed
Salt   1 teaspoon
Freshly ground pepper   1 teaspoon
Salad greens
Tomato slices   garnish

Mix together first 9 ingredients. Combine next 5 ingredients in a jar and pour over salad. Marinate in refrigerator at least 24 hours. Serve on greens with tomato slices. Serves 6 to 8.

Red Kidney Bean Salad

Red wine vinegar   ½ cup
Olive oil   7 tablespoons
Salt   1 teaspoon
Freshly ground pepper   to taste
Oregano   ½ teaspoon
Celery   ½ cup finely chopped
Onion   ¼ cup finely chopped
Red kidney beans   1 pound, cooked, or
   Canned red kidney beans   two 16-ounce cans, drained
Lettuce cups   8

Thoroughly mix first 7 ingredients and pour over beans. Marinate at room temperature at least 1 hour. Chill thoroughly and serve in lettuce cups. Serves 8.

Kidney Bean Salad

Small onion 1, chopped
Celery 4 stalks, chopped
Kidney beans 2 cups cooked
India Relish ¼ cup
Mayonnaise ¼ cup
Salt 1 teaspoon
Pepper ⅛ teaspoon
Lettuce

Put onion, celery, and beans in a bowl. Combine next 4 ingredients and stir into bean mixture. Chill well and serve on lettuce. Serves 4.

Lentil Salad

Lentils 8 ounces
Parsley 3 sprigs
Fresh thyme 2 sprigs or
   Dried thyme ½ teaspoon
Water 3 cups
Bay leaf ½
Garlic clove 1
Onion 2 tablespoons finely chopped
Salt and pepper to taste
Parsley 1 tablespoon finely chopped
Garlic ½ teaspoon finely minced
Tomatoes 1 tablespoon peeled, seeded, and diced
Red wine vinegar 1 tablespoon
Olive oil 3 tablespoons
Salad greens

Place lentils in saucepan. Tie together parsley and thyme sprigs and add to lentils with next 5 ingredients. Bring to a boil and cook, partially covered, about 30 minutes until lentils are barely tender. Remove garlic, parsley bundle, and bay leaf and discard. Drain lentils well and place in a large salad bowl. Add remaining ingredients and toss well. Chill and serve on a bed of greens. Serves 4 to 8.

Marinated Lentil Salad

Lentils   11 ounces
Water   2 cups
Large onion   1, finely chopped
Cayenne flakes   to taste
Olive oil   2 tablespoons
Garlic cloves   2, finely minced
Water   2 quarts
Salt   to taste
Bay leaves   2
Wine vinegar   3 tablespoons
Lemon juice   1 tablespoon
Olive oil   2 tablespoons
Salt and pepper   to taste
Dressing
Tomato wedges   garnish
Olives   garnish
Watercress or parsley sprigs   garnish

Soak lentils overnight or quick-soak, then drain. Remove 1 cup lentils and place them in 2 cups water. Add ½ the onion and a few flakes of cayenne. Simmer 1½ hours; cool. Place remaining lentils in a large pot. Sauté remaining onion in 2 tablespoons olive oil, then add to lentils in pot. Sauté garlic in same oil 1 to 2 minutes, then add garlic to lentils. Add water, salt, and bay leaves and simmer about 1½ hours until lentils are tender; cool. Combine the 2 lentil mixtures. Add vinegar, lemon juice, 2 tablespoons oil, and salt and pepper; marinate overnight. Pour dressing over lentils, chill well, and garnish. Serves 6 to 8.

Dressing

Large onion   ½, finely chopped
Fresh parsley   ½ to ⅔ cup chopped
Prepared mustard   1 teaspoon
Salt and pepper   to taste
Olive oil   3 tablespoons
Lemon juice   of 1 lemon

Thoroughly mix onion, parsley, mustard, and salt and pepper; slowly add oil, beating until mixture thickens. Add lemon juice and beat again. Makes ½ cup.

Cold Curried Lentils

Lentils 1½ cups
Water 3 cups
Medium onions 4, finely chopped
Butter ¼ cup
Curry powder 2 tablespoons
Beef bouillon 2 cups
Salt 2 teaspoons
Pepper ½ teaspoon
Lemon juice 1 tablespoon
Lettuce cups 6
Sour cream ½ cup

Soak lentils overnight or quick-soak; drain. Cook in 3 cups water until done but still firm; drain. Sauté onions in butter until soft, then stir in curry powder and cook over low heat 20 minutes, stirring frequently. Add bouillon, salt, pepper, and lentils. Cover and simmer very slowly about 3 hours until lentils are very soft. Chill thoroughly. Just before serving, mix in lemon juice. Serve in lettuce cups and top each serving with a dollop of sour cream. Serves 6.

German Sour Bean Salad

Lima beans 1 pound, cooked, or
    Canned lima beans three 17-ounce cans
Medium onion 1, thinly sliced and separated into rings
Sour cream 1 cup
Cider vinegar 2 tablespoons
Sugar 1 tablespoon
Prepared horseradish 1 teaspoon
Salt 2 teaspoons
White pepper ¼ teaspoon
Lettuce cups 6 to 8
Parsley ¼ cup chopped

Drain beans thoroughly; toss gently with onion rings. Mix next 6 ingredients and fold into bean mixture. Marinate at room temperature at least 1 hour. Chill, then spoon into lettuce cups and sprinkle with parsley. Serves 6 to 8.

Haricots Blancs

White navy beans 2 cups, cooked
White onions 2, peeled, thinly sliced, and separated into rings
Parsley ½ cup chopped
Vinaigrette Dressing ½ cup

Layer beans, onions, and parsley in a bowl. Pour dressing over salad and refrigerate overnight to blend flavors. Serves 6 to 8.

Vinaigrette Dressing

Vinegar 1 tablespoon
Olive or safflower oil 3 tablespoons
Salt and pepper to taste

Combine all ingredients and use as a marinade. Makes ¼ cup.

Beans Primavera

Navy beans or white beans 1 pound or
    Canned cannellini beans three 16-ounce cans, drained
Whole cloves 2
Onion 1
Water
Solid-style tuna two 6½-ounce cans, drained
Garlic cloves 3, minced
Parsley ¼ cup finely chopped
Fresh basil ¼ cup finely chopped
Wine vinegar to taste
Olive oil to taste
Salt and pepper to taste
Parsley garnish
Toast or crackers (optional)

If using dried beans, soak overnight or quick-soak; drain. Insert cloves halfway into onion, and put into a pot with beans. Cover with water and cook until beans are tender but not mushy. Discard onion and drain beans. Break tuna into pieces. Mix with garlic, parsley, and basil, then add to beans. Add vinegar, oil, salt, and pepper and fold together (this should be done while beans are still hot). Chill well. Sprinkle with parsley and serve either as a salad, or as a main course spooned on crisp toast or crackers. Serves 10.

Bean–Rice Confetti Salad

Brown rice 1 cup cooked and chilled
Pinto or pink beans 1⅔ cups cooked or
   Canned pinto or pink beans 15-ounce can, drained
Dill pickles ¼ cup chopped
Green pepper ¼ cup chopped
Celery ¼ cup chopped
Green onion 2 tablespoons chopped
Carrot ¼ cup shredded
Freshly ground pepper dash
Mayonnaise ⅓ cup
Eggs 4, hard-cooked and sliced
Salad greens
Chopped parsley topping
Carrot curls garnish
Dill pickle wedges garnish
Hard-cooked egg slices garnish

Mix together first 10 ingredients and place in salad bowl lined with greens. Sprinkle with parsley and garnish with carrot curls, pickle wedges, and egg slices. Serves 4 to 6.

Pink and Red Salad

Pinto beans 4 cups cooked or
    Canned pinto beans two 15-ounce cans, drained
Red cabbage 2 cups finely shredded
Celery 1 cup finely chopped
Radishes 1 cup finely chopped
Cucumbers 1 cup seeded and finely chopped
Onion ¼ cup finely chopped
Oil 1 cup
Cider vinegar ¼ cup
Mayonnaise ½ cup
Salt 1½ teaspoons
Pepper ⅛ teaspoon
Dry mustard ⅛ teaspoon
Salad greens

Combine first 6 ingredients in a large bowl. Combine remaining ingredients except greens in a blender and whirl until well mixed. Pour dressing over vegetable mixture and toss until vegetables are well coated. Cover and refrigerate several hours. Toss again; serve on greens. Serves 8.

Texas Bean Salad

Pinto or kidney beans or garbanzos, singly or mixed 2 cups cooked
Onion 1, thinly sliced
Garlic cloves 2, minced
Green pepper ½, sliced
Cider vinegar ¼ cup
Salad oil ⅓ cup
Salt 1 teaspoon
Lettuce

Put beans in a large bowl and add remaining ingredients except lettuce. Marinate 1 to 2 hours at room temperature. Chill, if desired, and serve on lettuce. Serves 4.

Cannellini Bean Salad

Bread   1 slice
Garlic cloves   2, minced
Walnuts   ⅓ cup
Chicken broth   1 cup
Salt   ½ teaspoon
Pepper   ½ teaspoon
Tabasco sauce   dash
Lemon juice   1 tablespoon
Cannellini beans (white beans) or navy beans   1 pound, cooked, or
   Canned cannellini beans   two 16-ounce cans, drained
Salad greens
Chopped parsley   garnish
Chopped mint   garnish

In a blender, whirl bread into fine crumbs. Add next 7 ingredients and blend at high speed about 1 minute. Pour over beans and mix to coat well. Serve on greens and sprinkle with parsley and mint. Serves 6.

Cannellini Beans with Tuna

Cannellini beans (white beans)   5 to 6 cups cooked or
   Canned cannellini beans   three 16-ounce cans, drained
Scallions or onion   ¼ cup finely chopped
Garlic   ½ teaspoon finely minced
Dried oregano   ½ teaspoon crumbled
Parsley   2 tablespoons finely chopped
Red wine vinegar   1 tablespoon
Lemon juice   of ½ lemon
Olive oil   ¼ cup
Salt and pepper   to taste
Tuna packed in oil   two 6½-ounce cans, drained
Salad greens
Tomato slices   garnish

Put beans in salad bowl and add next 8 ingredients. Flake tuna into large chunks; toss with bean mixture. Place on greens and garnish with tomatoes. Serves 4 to 6.

Spinach–Bean Salad

Cider vinegar ⅓ cup
Oil 3 tablespoons
Salt 1 teaspoon
Sugar ½ teaspoon
Ground thyme ½ teaspoon
Basil ½ teaspoon
Pepper ¼ teaspoon
Garlic clove 1, minced
White beans 2 to 3 cups cooked or
    Canned cannellini beans 2 to 3 cups, drained
Celery 1 cup sliced
Parsley ½ cup chopped
Medium onion 1, thinly sliced and separated into rings
Oil 2 tablespoons
Spinach 8 ounces, stems removed, and shredded
Pimiento 1, cut into strips

In a salad bowl, thoroughly mix first 8 ingredients. Add beans and let stand at least 2 hours to marinate. Add celery, parsley, and onion and let stand 30 minutes more. Stir to blend. (At this point, mixture may be refrigerated overnight, if desired; bring to room temperature before proceeding with recipe.) Sprinkle oil over spinach; add to bean mixture and toss gently. Garnish with pimiento. Serves 4.

Soups and Stews

Any-Bean Soup

Any beans 4 cups cooked, undrained
Meat or chicken stock 2 cups
Lime juice 2 tablespoons
Small onions 2, finely chopped
Chili powder 2 teaspoons
Salt to taste
Yogurt or sour cream garnish

Simmer all ingredients except yogurt until beans are tender but firm. Garnish with plain yogurt or sour cream. Serves 4.

Spanish Bean-and-Garlic Soup

Water 6 cups
Any beans 2 cups
Small garlic cloves 8, minced
Salt 2 teaspoons
Olive oil 1 tablespoon (optional)

In 6 cups water, soak beans overnight or quick-soak. Bring to a boil, then add garlic and salt and simmer until beans are tender. Add oil just before serving. Serves 4 to 6.

Make-Believe Turtle Soup

Black beans 1½ cups cooked
Regular strength beef broth 14½-ounce can
Deviled ham half 2¼-ounce can
Pastina ¼ cup, uncooked
Dry sherry 2 tablespoons

Mix beans, broth, and ham in a saucepan. Stir well, then add pastina. Simmer about 10 minutes until the pasta is just tender; add sherry and serve immediately. Serves 2 to 3.

Mayan Bean Soup

Bacon   4 strips
Black beans or Mexican brown beans   2 cups cooked
Corn   ½ cup, cooked
Garlic powder   dash
Taco sauce or salsa picante   1 tablespoon
Water

Fry bacon strips and crumble; reserve drippings. Mix beans, corn, and garlic powder in a saucepan. Add water to thin, and drippings as desired for flavor. Cook and stir over medium heat until hot. Sprinkle with bacon crumbles and serve. Serves 2 to 3.

Broiled Black Bean Soup

Garlic clove   1, minced
Butter or margarine   1 tablespoon
Black Bean Soup   1 quart or
    Condensed black bean soup   10½-ounce can*
Lemon juice   1 tablespoon
Green onions   ¼ cup chopped
Whipping cream   ½ cup, beaten until stiff
Lemon peel   1 teaspoon
Salt   ¼ teaspoon
Pepper   dash

Sauté garlic in butter until golden. Add soup and lemon juice. Heat but *do not* boil. Stir in green onions; ladle into 4 oven-proof soup bowls. Stir together remaining ingredients. Float cream mixture on top of soup and broil about 6 inches from heat until golden brown. Serve immediately. Serves 4.
* If using canned soup, add 1¼ cups water.

Black Bean Soup

Black beans*   1½ cups
Water   3 quarts
Large onion   1, chopped
Salt   to taste
Oil   2 tablespoons
Tortillas   3
Shortening or oil   for frying
Summer savory   one 3-inch piece
Tomato puree   3 tablespoons
Small garlic clove   1, minced
Parsley   2 tablespoons chopped
Chili powder   to taste
Shredded cheese   topping

Soak beans overnight or quick-soak; discard floating beans, then drain. In a large pot, cook beans in water with onion, salt, and oil, boiling gently until beans are very soft. Drain, reserving liquid. Mash beans or puree in a blender or food processor. Fry tortillas lightly in shortening; remove from pan. Add sausage to shortening in pan and fry lightly. Remove and set aside. Combine tomato puree, garlic, parsley, and chili powder, and add to mashed beans and liquid, adding stock or water to thin if needed. Adjust seasonings to taste and heat for 10 to 15 minutes. Before serving add cut-up tortillas and sausage and top with cheese. Serves 8.
* Mexican brown beans may be substituted for black beans.

Maria's Black Bean Soup

Water 1 quart
Black beans 1 cup
Oil 2 tablespoons
Onions 2, sliced
Celery 2 stalks, sliced
Salt ½ teaspoon
Bay leaf 1
Celery seed 1 teaspoon
Basil ¼ teaspoon
Lemon juice of ½ lemon
Soy sauce 1 tablespoon
Parsley, hard-cooked egg slices, or thin lemon slices garnish

In 1 quart water, soak beans overnight or quick-soak. Heat oil in uncovered pressure cooker and sauté onions and celery until tender. Add
beans and soaking water and pressure-cook for 1½ hours, or until beans
are very tender. Puree bean mixture in blender, food mill, or food processor. Return to stove. Add next 4 ingredients and simmer 15 minutes.
(At this point the mixture may be thickened if desired by adding 2 tablespoons of flour and cooking an additional 15 minutes.) Add lemon juice
and soy sauce; heat thoroughly. Remove bay leaf. Garnish with parsley,
egg slices, or lemon slices and serve. Serves 3 to 4.

Cuban Black Bean Soup

Black beans 1 pound
Olive oil 2 tablespoons
Lean salt pork 4 ounces, cut into small cubes
Onion 2 cups finely chopped
Garlic 1 tablespoon finely minced
Green pepper 1½ cups finely chopped
Beef broth or water 2 quarts
Bay leaf 1
Oregano 1 teaspoon
Smoked ham hocks 1½ pounds
Dried red peppers 1 or 2
Salt and pepper to taste
Wine vinegar 2 tablespoons
Dry sherry ¼ cup (optional)
Cooked rice 12 servings
Chopped onions or scallions, or lemon slices garnish

Soak beans overnight or quick-soak; drain. Heat oil in a large kettle and add salt pork, stirring often to render fat. Add onions, garlic, and green pepper and cook until vegetables are soft. Add beans and next 6 ingredients. Bring mixture to a boil, then reduce heat and simmer 2 to 3 hours, or until beans are quite soft. Remove bay leaf and discard. Remove ham hocks from kettle; remove meat from bones and chop finely. Puree bean mixture and return to kettle; add vinegar and sherry and heat thoroughly. Serve with rice, garnish with onions, scallions, or lemon slices, and sprinkle with chopped meat from the ham hocks. Serves 12.

Haitian Black Bean Soup

Black beans   2 cups
Water
Salt   1 tablespoon
Olive oil   2 tablespoons
Medium onions   2, chopped
Garlic cloves   3, minced
Hot water   1 cup
Ham   8 ounces, cut into small cubes
Chicken broth   1 quart
Tomatoes   16-ounce can, chopped
White vinegar   2 tablespoons
Ground cumin   ½ teaspoon
Freshly ground pepper   to taste
Tabasco sauce   generous dash
Thinly sliced bananas   garnish (optional)

In a large Dutch oven, cover beans with water and add salt; soak overnight or quick-soak. Bring beans to a boil, then reduce heat to low and partially cover. Simmer about 3 hours until beans are tender, adding more boiling water as needed. Drain and set aside. Put oil, onions, garlic, and water in the Dutch oven and bring to a boil. When onions are transparent and water has evaporated, stir in beans and remaining ingredients except bananas. Bring to a boil; simmer, stirring frequently, about 15 minutes until beans are thoroughly warmed. Garnish with sliced bananas if desired. Serves 6 to 8.

Cranberry Bean Minestrone

Cranberry beans   1 cup
Minestrone Stock (see Index)   11 cups
Water   2½ cups
Long grain rice   ½ cup
Carrots   4, sliced
Large new potatoes   2, peeled and cut into ½-inch cubes
Large tomatoes   2, chopped
Cabbage   1 small head, coarsely shredded
Medium zucchini   4, cut into ½-inch slices
Ham reserved from stock
Grated Parmesan cheese
Pesto Sauce (see Index)

Soak beans overnight or quick-soak; drain. Bring stock to a boil; add beans and water and simmer 2 hours, or until beans are easily mashed. Spoon out ⅔ of the beans and enough liquid to puree in a blender, then return to stock. Bring to a boil; add rice, carrots, potatoes, and tomatoes. Cover and simmer 15 minutes. Add cabbage and zucchini and simmer 5 to 10 minutes more. Add ham and heat thoroughly. Serve at room temperature or hot, topped with Parmesan cheese and Pesto Sauce. Serves 6 to 8.

Potage Musard

Flageolets   1 pound
Cloves   2
Onion   1
Water   3 quarts
Salt   to taste
Carrot   1, peeled
Bay leaf   1
Fresh thyme   2 sprigs
Milk   ½ cup
Heavy cream   ½ cup
Butter   ¼ cup
Freshly ground pepper   to taste
Croutons

Soak beans overnight or quick-soak; drain. Place beans in a kettle. Insert cloves halfway into onion and add to beans with next 5 ingredients. Bring to a boil, cover, and simmer about 1½ hours until tender. Remove from heat. Remove 1 cup of beans and reserve. Remove bay leaf and discard. Cool remaining bean mixture, then puree in a food mill or processor. Return to kettle; add milk, cream, and reserved beans. Bring to a boil; add butter and stir. Adjust salt to taste; add pepper. Serve with hot croutons. Serves 10 to 12.

Garbanzo–Chorizo Soup

Ham shank 2 pounds, cut into pieces
Water 3 quarts
Large onions 2, sliced
Bay leaf 1
Beef bouillon cubes 2
Chorizo 1 pound, cut into ½-inch slices
Garlic cloves 4 to 6, thinly sliced
Garbanzos 4 cups cooked or
    Canned garbanzos two 16-ounce cans, drained
Cabbage ½ small head, coarsely shredded
Large carrots 4, cut into ¼-inch slices
Green peppers 2, seeded and cut into ¼-inch slices
Salt and pepper to taste
Tabasco sauce

In a large kettle, combine first 5 ingredients and simmer about 1½ hours until meat is tender. Remove ham shank. Cut meat into bite-sized pieces and add to soup; discard bone. Brown sausage with garlic; add to soup with 1 tablespoon of the drippings. Add next 5 ingredients and simmer about 20 minutes until carrots and peppers are tender. Skim off fat and serve. Pass Tabasco sauce at the table. Serves 6 to 8.

Puré de Garbanzos

Garbanzos   1 pound
Medium onion   1
Small carrots   2
Bacon strips   2
Beef broth   3 cups
Hierbas de olor*
Salt   to taste

Soak garbanzos overnight or quick-soak; drain. Cook garbanzos with next 5 ingredients over low heat about 4 hours until garbanzos are completely soft, stirring frequently to prevent sticking and adding more broth if needed. Lift out the bacon and vegetables and chop. Discard hierbas de olor. Puree garbanzos, then return to pot with bacon, carrots, and onion. Add salt and reheat. Add broth if puree is too thick. Serves 4.
* Mexican herb bouquet consisting of 1 bay leaf and a sprig each of thyme, oregano, and marjoram tied to make a secure bundle.

Sopa de Vigilia (Soup for the Fast Days)

Garbanzos   1 cup
Dried codfish   8 ounces
Water   2 quarts
Carrots   2
Onion   1, quartered
Salt and pepper   to taste
Onion   1, chopped
Garlic cloves   2, minced
Spinach   2 bunches, chopped
Olive oil   ¼ cup
Tomatoes   2 cups chopped
Ground thyme   ¼ teaspoon
Marjoram   ¼ teaspoon
Ground oregano   ½ teaspoon
Parsley   1 sprig
Bay leaves   2
Chopped hard-cooked eggs   topping

Soak garbanzos and codfish overnight in separate bowls; drain. Separate codfish into small chunks and put in a pot with garbanzos and next 4 ingredients. Cook for 4 hours, then remove from heat. Mash or puree one carrot and 3 tablespoons of the garbanzos. Discard remaining carrot and the onion. In a frying pan sauté chopped onion, garlic, and spinach in oil until onion is tender and spinach is wilted. Add next 4 ingredients and cook 5 minutes more. Add tomato mixture, mashed carrot and garbanzos, parsley, and bay leaves to garbanzos and cook 15 minutes. Remove bay leaves, sprinkle eggs on soup, and serve. Serves 8.

Lenten Convent Soup

Garbanzos or lima beans 8 ounces
Water 2 quarts
Baking soda pinch
Water
Onion 1
Bay leaf 1
Parsley 1 sprig
Cloves 2
Onion 1, chopped
Olive oil 3 tablespoons
Egg yolks 3, hard-cooked
Salt and pepper to taste

Soak garbanzos overnight or quick-soak; drain. Boil garbanzos in 2 quarts water for 1 hour. Add soda and boil until skins loosen; drain, reserving liquid. Remove skins. Cover garbanzos with water. Add onion, bay leaf, parsley, and cloves; cover and cook until onion is tender. Remove onion, bay leaf, parsley, and cloves, and discard. Sauté chopped onion in olive oil until golden; remove ½ the garbanzos from stock and add them to onion and oil. Add egg yolks and mash them well, adding bean liquid as needed. Add egg mixture to soup and cook until garbanzos are tender. Serves 8.

Spinach and Garbanzo Soup

Beef broth 2 quarts
Garbanzos 2 cups cooked or
   Canned garbanzos 16-ounce can, drained
Carrots 1 cup chopped
Onion 1 cup chopped
Celery 1 cup chopped
Turnip 1 cup chopped
Spinach 1 cup coarsely chopped
Stewed tomatoes 16-ounce can
Grated Parmesan cheese topping

Simmer first 6 ingredients for 30 minutes. Add spinach and tomatoes and simmer 10 minutes more. Serve with Parmesan cheese. Serves 4 to 6.

Mulligatawny Soup

Fryer chickens 2, cut into serving-sized pieces
Water 2 quarts
Salt 1 tablespoon
Butter 6 tablespoons
Turmeric 4½ teaspoons
Poppy seeds 3 tablespoons
Coriander 3 tablespoons
Cayenne dash
Coconut ½ cup
Medium onion 1, finely chopped
Garlic cloves 3 or 4, minced
Flour 1 cup
Garbanzos 2 cups cooked
Butter 2 tablespoons
Cloves 4 or 5
Salt to taste
Cayenne to taste
Hot cooked rice
Lemon slices

Put chicken, water, and salt in a pot; bring to a boil, then simmer about 1 hour until chicken is tender. Remove chicken from pot, cool, and remove meat from bones. Reserve stock. Melt butter in 2 cups chicken stock; add next 7 ingredients and cook until onion is soft. Remove from heat and stir in flour. Puree garbanzos and add to soup. Add chicken stock, if needed, and meat; simmer 15 minutes. Melt butter with cloves. Just before serving, remove cloves and add butter to soup. Add salt and cayenne. Serve with rice and lemon slices. Serves 8 to 10.

Garbanzo Soup

Garbanzos 2 cups
Water
Salt to taste
Dried rosemary ½ teaspoon
Olive oil 2 tablespoons
Onion 3 tablespoons chopped
Garlic cloves 3, crushed or minced
Green chili peppers 3 tablespoons chopped
Worcestershire sauce 1 tablespoon
Tomato paste ¼ cup
Freshly ground pepper
Shell macaroni 1 cup
French bread

Cover garbanzos with water and soak overnight or quick-soak. Add more water if necessary and cook until garbanzos are tender. Add salt, rosemary, and more water if needed, and simmer while preparing next 6 ingredients for addition to the soup. Heat olive oil in a small saucepan and add onion and garlic; cook until onion is transparent. Add peppers, Worcestershire sauce, and tomato paste, then add this mixture to beans. Season with pepper and adjust salt to taste. Add enough water to make room for the macaroni. Bring to a boil, then add macaroni. Continue cooking until macaroni is tender. Serve hot with French bread. Serves 6 to 8.

Garbanzo Pottage

Garbanzos   1 pound
Water
Whole cloves   2
Medium onion   1
Bay leaves   2
Parsley   1 sprig
Medium onion   1, chopped
Oil   2 tablespoons
Egg yolks   3 hard-cooked
Salt and pepper   to taste

Cover garbanzos with water and soak overnight or quick-soak. Insert cloves halfway into onion; put in pot with garbanzos, bay leaves, and parsley. Cook until garbanzos are tender. Drain, reserving liquid; remove skins. Remove bay leaves and parsley, and discard. Sauté chopped onion in oil. Remove cloves from cooked onion; finely chop the onion and add to sautéed onion. Grind in a food processor or finely chop the egg yolks and ½ the garbanzos; stir into bean liquid and add whole garbanzos and onion mixture. Add salt and pepper. This is traditionally served with fried bread. Serves 4 to 5.

Kidney Bean and Lamb Soup

Water   3 cups
Red kidney beans   1 cup
Large lamb shank   1
Butter   2 tablespoons
Large onion   1, finely chopped
Celery   1 large stalk, finely chopped
Medium carrot   1, finely chopped
Garlic clove   1, minced
Tomato juice   1 cup
Salt   3 teaspoons
Pepper   ¼ teaspoon
Bay leaf   1
Ground cloves   ¼ teaspoon
Thyme leaves   ¼ teaspoon crumbled
Lemon juice   2 teaspoons

In 3 cups water, soak beans overnight or quick-soak. Drain bean liquid and reserve; add enough water to make 6 cups. In a Dutch oven, brown lamb shank in butter. Add onion, celery, carrot, and garlic; sauté until vegetables are tender. Add remaining ingredients except lemon juice; bring to a boil. Reduce heat, cover, and simmer 1½ hours, or until meat is tender. Remove shank from soup; cool slightly, then remove meat from bone. Cut meat into small pieces and return to soup. Remove bay leaf. Stir in lemon juice, adjust seasonings to taste, and serve. Serves 6 to 8.

Black Rice Soup

Kidney beans 4 cups cooked or
    Canned kidney beans two 16-ounce cans, drained
Shortening 1 tablespoon
Onion 1 tablespoon chopped
Rice ½ cup
Tomato sauce ½ cup
Salt and pepper to taste
Water 2 quarts

Mash beans or puree in blender. In a large pot, melt shortening and add onion and washed rice. When rice begins to brown, add tomato sauce, salt, and pepper and cook 10 minutes. Add beans and water; simmer until rice is tender and soup is creamy. Serves 8.

Lentil Soup

Lentils 2 cups
Onions 2, finely chopped
Carrots 2, finely chopped
Turnip 1, finely chopped
Celery 3 stalks, finely chopped
Beef or chicken stock 6 cups
Pepper dash
Salt to taste
Flour or cornstarch (optional)

Place all ingredients except flour in a pot; bring to a boil, then simmer about 1½ hours. Thicken with flour if desired. Serves 4.

Lentil Soup with Noodles

Lentils 1½ cups
Water 2 quarts
Chicken bouillon cubes 4
Medium onions 2, finely chopped
Olive oil ½ cup
Garlic cloves 3, minced
Fresh coriander 1 teaspoon chopped (optional)
Wide egg noodles 3 ounces
Salt and pepper to taste
Chopped fresh coriander garnish

Combine lentils and water in a pot and bring to a boil; add bouillon cubes and stir until they are dissolved. Reduce heat and simmer 40 minutes, or until lentils are tender. Meanwhile, sauté onions in oil over medium heat until golden; add garlic and coriander to onions just before they are done. Add onion mixture to soup. Add noodles to soup 10 minutes before lentils are done, and add more water if necessary. Season with salt and pepper and garnish with coriander. Serves 4 to 6.
Variation: Browned and sliced "hard" or winter sausage or frankfurters may be added to this soup to give it additional heartiness.

Creamy Lentil Soup

Lentils 1 cup
Water 1 quart
Large potato 1, peeled and finely chopped
Small onion 1, finely chopped
Butter 2 tablespoons
Beef bouillon cubes 2
Chicken bouillon cubes 2
Light cream or milk ½ cup
Hot buttered croutons

Put lentils and water in a 3-quart kettle. Bring to a boil, then add potato and simmer about 45 minutes until potato is very soft. Sauté onion in butter until golden brown and add to lentils. Add bouillon cubes and stir until they are dissolved; remove from heat. Pour ⅓ of the lentil mixture at a time into a blender and blend until smooth; return blended mixture to kettle and stir in cream. If the mixture seems too thick, add hot milk or boiling water to achieve the desired consistency. Top with hot buttered croutons and serve. Serves 4 to 6.

Lebanese Lentil Soup with Lemon

Lentils 1½ cups
Water 7 to 8 cups
Beef bouillon cubes 4
Medium potato 1, peeled and cut into 1½-inch cubes
Swiss chard 2 bunches (about 1½ pounds), cut into strips
Medium onion 1, finely chopped
Olive oil 6 tablespoons
Fresh coriander 1 bunch or
    Dried coriander 2 tablespoons
Garlic cloves 3, minced
Salt ¾ teaspoon
Pepper ¼ teaspoon
Ground cumin ½ teaspoon
Lemon juice 3 tablespoons
Lemon slices garnish

In a large kettle combine lentils and water. Add bouillon cubes and cover; bring to a boil, then simmer. Add potato and chard; cover and simmer 40 minutes, or until lentils are tender. Sauté onion in oil until soft and golden; set aside. Reserve ¼ of the coriander for garnish and add remainder with garlic and sautéed onion to lentils during last 5 minutes of cooking. Stir in next 4 ingredients and add water if needed to thin soup. Garnish with reserved coriander and lemon slices, and serve. Serves 8 to 10.

Greek Lentil Soup

Lentils 2 cups
Vegetable stock or water 6 cups
Onion ½, chopped
Small carrot 1, chopped
Celery 1 stalk, chopped
Oil 2 tablespoons
Small potato 1, chopped
Bay leaves 2
Salt 1½ teaspoons
Vinegar 2 teaspoons

Mix all ingredients except vinegar in a soup pot; bring to a boil, then reduce heat and simmer until lentils are soft. Add vinegar, remove bay leaves, and serve. Serves 4.

Sausage–Lentil Soup

Onion   ½ cup chopped
Butter   2 tablespoons
Water   8½ cups
Lentils   1 pound
Polish sausage   1 pound, cut into bite-sized pieces
Salt   1 teaspoon or to taste
Frozen chopped spinach   half 10-ounce package, thawed, or
   Fresh spinach   6 cups torn
Lemon juice   1 tablespoon

In a Dutch oven, sauté onion in butter until lightly browned. Add water, lentils, sausage, and salt and bring to a boil; skim off foam. Lower heat, cover, and simmer about 40 minutes until lentils are tender. Stir in spinach and continue cooking until spinach is wilted. Add lemon juice. Serves 8.
Note: This soup freezes well.

Escarole–Lentil Soup

Onions   1 cup chopped
Garlic clove   1, minced
Parsley   2 tablespoons chopped
Olive oil   3 tablespoons
Water   6 cups
Lentils   1 pound
Escarole   1 small head (about 1 pound), shredded
Salt   2 teaspoons or to taste
Freshly ground pepper   ½ teaspoon
Parmesan cheese   ½ cup grated

In a Dutch oven over medium heat stir onions, garlic, and parsley in oil for 5 minutes. Add water and lentils and bring to a boil; cover and simmer 1 hour, or until lentils are tender. Add escarole, salt, and pepper and simmer 10 minutes more, or until escarole is wilted. Add more water if desired. Serve hot, topped with Parmesan cheese. Serves 4 to 6.

Cream of Lentil Soup

Cloves 2
Onion 1
Lentils 1 cup
Water 1 quart
Ham bone 1
Celery with leaves ½ cup chopped
Carrot 1, chopped
Potato 1, chopped
Milk 3½ cups
Salt to taste
Cayenne ½ teaspoon
Well-seasoned salami 4 ounces, chopped

Insert cloves halfway into onion. Put in a pot with next 6 ingredients; bring to a boil, cover, and simmer slowly about 2½ hours until lentils are soft. Remove ham bone and cloves; puree lentils and vegetables. Return pureed mixture to pot; add milk, salt, and cayenne, and simmer without boiling for 15 minutes. Serve hot with salami sprinkled on top. Serves 6.

Lentil and Bacon Soup

Lentils 4 ounces
Water 3 cups
Salt and pepper to taste
Bacon 3 strips, finely chopped
Onions 2, finely chopped
Tomato sauce 8-ounce can
Beef or chicken stock 2 quarts
Egg yolks 2
Pimientos ¼ cup cut into strips

Soak lentils in water with salt and pepper for 1 hour; drain. Fry bacon lightly and remove from pan. Sauté onions in bacon fat until just golden. Add tomato sauce and simmer 10 minutes. Add lentils, bacon, and stock and simmer 45 minutes more; remove from heat. Beat egg yolks into 1 cup of the soup, then add to soup. Stir in pimientos and serve immediately. Serves 8.

Beef and Lentil Soup

Meaty beef bones 4 pounds, cut into 4-inch chunks
Bay leaves 2
Water 3 quarts
Salt 3½ teaspoons
Ground thyme 1 teaspoon
Tomatoes 16-ounce can, quartered
Lentils ¾ cup
Large carrots 2, peeled and chopped
Fresh green beans 8 ounces, cut into ½-inch pieces
Cabbage 1 cup coarsely chopped
Grated Parmesan cheese

Place bones, bay leaves, water, and salt in a large kettle. Bring to a boil, then reduce heat, cover, and simmer 3 hours, or until meat drops easily from bones. Pour broth through a sieve and return liquid to pan. Remove meat from bones and cut into bite-sized pieces. Put meat in broth; discard bones and bay leaves. Add next 5 ingredients to broth. Bring to a boil; reduce heat and simmer 20 minutes. Remove from heat and skim off foam. Add cabbage to broth and simmer 3 minutes more. Adjust seasonings to taste and serve with Parmesan cheese. Makes 3 quarts.

Creole Lentil Soup

Boiling water 2 quarts
Lentils 1 cup
Salt 1½ teaspoons
Butter 3 tablespoons
Onion 1, chopped
Celery 1 stalk, chopped
Small green pepper 1, seeded and chopped
Small sweet red pepper 1, seeded and chopped
Brewer's yeast ½ teaspoon (optional)
Vegetable broth powder 1 teaspoon
Brown sugar 1 teaspoon
Bay leaf 1
Catsup or tomato puree 2 tablespoons
Flour 2 tablespoons
Freshly ground pepper to taste

Pour boiling water over lentils, cover, and let stand about 1 hour, then add salt. Melt butter in a frying pan; add chopped vegetables and brewer's yeast and sauté until vegetables are tender. Add sautéed mixture and next 3 ingredients to lentils and cook over low heat 1½ to 2 hours. Mix the catsup or tomato puree with flour and slowly add to soup, stirring constantly. Add pepper. Continue stirring over low heat about 5 to 10 minutes until flour mixture is cooked. Serve with more freshly ground pepper. Serves 6 to 8.

Blonde Lentil Soup

Celery 3 stalks, cut into large pieces
Medium carrots 5, thickly sliced
Large onion 1, quartered
Monosodium glutamate to taste
Water 5 cups
Shallots 3, chopped
Onion 1, chopped
Garlic cloves 1 to 3, minced
Butter 2 tablespoons
Lemon peel 1 teaspoon grated
Bay leaf 1
Champagne lentils 1 cup
Lemon juice of 1 lemon
Sweet basil to taste
Salt and pepper to taste

Cook first 4 ingredients in water until vegetables are very tender. Discard celery and onion; press carrots through a sieve and return to stock. Sauté shallots, onions, and garlic in butter until light brown, then add them to stock. Add lemon peel, bay leaf, and lentils and cook gently 40 to 60 minutes, adding water as necessary to maintain the original consistency. When lentils are tender, remove bay leaf and add lemon juice, basil, and salt and pepper. Simmer 20 minutes, then serve. Serves 4.

Lentil or Split Pea Soup

Lentils or split peas   1½ cups
Whole cloves   2
Large onion   1
Chicken or beef stock or water   2 quarts
Bay leaf   1
Garlic cloves   2
Salt   pinch
Freshly ground pepper   to taste
Crisply fried croutons   topping
Sour cream   topping

Soak lentils overnight or quick-soak; drain. Insert cloves halfway into onion. Put into large pot with lentils and next 5 ingredients. Bring to a boil, skim off foam, then simmer until lentils are well cooked. Remove bay leaf, garlic, and onion. Adjust seasonings to taste and serve. Soup may be pureed if desired, and each serving may be topped with croutons and/or a dollop of sour cream. Serve hot or cold. Serves 4 to 6.
Variations:
    Serve with sliced frankfurters or knackwurst and top with parsley.
    Top with sour cream or yogurt and chopped onions.
    Top with chopped tomatoes, chives, and thyme.
    Top with dollops of cooked rice.
    Top with chopped ham.

Louisiana Hot Bean Porridge

Water   3 quarts
Baby lima beans*   2 cups
Water   2 cups
Pearl barley   1 cup
Tomato sauce   8-ounce can
Onion   1 cup chopped
Garlic cloves   2, minced
Black peppercorns   12
Parsley   3 sprigs
Bay leaf   1
Worcestershire sauce   1 tablespoon
Ham   1 pound, cut into ½-inch cubes
Salt   2 teaspoons
Gumbo filé   1 teaspoon

Bring 3 quarts water to a boil and add beans. Return to boiling, then remove from heat, cover, and allow to soak overnight. Pour 2 cups water over barley and soak overnight. Drain barley and add with tomato sauce, onions, and garlic to beans and their liquid. Tie peppercorns, parsley, and bay leaf in a cheesecloth bag and add to bean mixture. Bring to a boil; reduce heat and simmer 1 hour. Remove 1 cup of bean and barley mixture with about ½ cup of liquid and blend until smooth. Add remaining ingredients to this mixture and return to the pot. Mix well and simmer 1 hour more. Makes 5½ quarts.

* Other beans may be substituted for lima beans.

Jewish Bean, Vegetable, and Noodle Soup

Jumbo marrow beans 1 cup
Beef or chicken stock or soup 7 cups
Medium onion 1, chopped
Celery ½ cup coarsely chopped
Small green pepper 1, seeded and chopped
Oil ¼ cup
Parsley 1 tablespoon chopped
Salt 1 tablespoon
Pepper dash
Garlic powder dash
Canned tomatoes or tomato juice 1 cup
Noodle squares (Plaetchen) ½ cup

Soak beans overnight or quick-soak; drain. In a large soup kettle, combine beans and stock and bring to a boil; reduce heat and simmer, covered, until beans are tender but still firm. Sauté onion, celery, and green pepper in oil for 5 minutes, stirring well. Add to soup with remaining ingredients; simmer 35 minutes more. Adjust seasonings to taste. Soup will thicken if not served immediately; add more stock, if necessary, to reach desired consistency. Serves 8.

Navy Bean Health Soup

Water or stock   2 quarts
White navy beans   2 cups
Celery with leaves   1 cup chopped
Carrots   1 cup chopped
Onions   1 to 2, chopped
Parsley   3 tablespoons chopped
Safflower oil   ¼ cup
Salt and pepper   to taste
Bay leaf   1
Small whole cayenne   1
Caraway seeds   1 teaspoon ground
Brewer's yeast   3 tablespoons
Minced chives   garnish

In 2 quarts of water or stock, soak beans overnight or quick-soak. In a large pot, combine all ingredients except chives; bring to a boil, cover, and simmer until beans and vegetables are tender. Add more stock or water as needed to reach desired consistency. Garnish with chives. Serves 6 to 8.

Puré de Legumbres

Navy beans   2 quarts
Water
Large onion   1, chopped
Oil
Large ripe tomato   1, peeled and chopped
Cornstarch   1 teaspoon
Water
Spinach, chard, or turnip greens   1 pound, chopped
Salt and pepper   to taste

Cover beans with water and soak overnight or quick-soak. Cook until skins are loose; drain, reserving liquid. Remove skins and puree the beans. Sauté onion in oil until golden, then add tomato. Mix cornstarch with a little water and add to onion mixture. Stir into bean puree. Add bean liquid, spinach, and salt and pepper. Cover and simmer 30 minutes. Serve with red salsa and hot garlic bread or rolls. Serves 8.

Garbure Basquaise

White navy beans   1 pound
Dried peas   8 ounces
Water   3 quarts
Whole cloves   2
Onion   1
Meaty ham hock or knuckle   1
Bay leaves   2
Salt   pinch
Potatoes   6, cut into 1-inch cubes
Carrots   4 or 5, sliced
Turnips   4, cut into ½-inch cubes
Leeks   4 or 5, sliced
Garlic cloves   6, minced
Bay leaf   1
Ground thyme   1 teaspoon
Cabbage   1 small head, shredded
Sausage links   12 to 16, cooked
Shredded Swiss cheese   topping (optional)

Soak beans and peas overnight or quick-soak; drain. Put beans, peas, and water in a deep kettle. Insert cloves into onion and add to beans with ham hock, bay leaves, and salt. Cook until beans are just tender, adjusting salt to taste. Drain, reserving liquid; discard onion and bay leaves. Cover beans and set aside in a warm oven. In the bean liquid, cook next 7 ingredients until vegetables are tender; add cabbage, sausage, beans, and the lean meat from the ham hock. The soup will be very thick; it can be served directly from the kettle, or place it in an ovenproof casserole, top with Swiss cheese, and melt cheese under a broiler. Serves 6 to 8.

Jewish Bean-and-Barley Soup

Water   2 quarts
Navy beans   1 cup
Beef chuck   1 pound
Beef flank   1 pound
Medium-fine barley   ½ cup
Carrots   3, peeled and sliced
Celery   2 large stalks, sliced
Medium onion   1, sliced
Ginger   ⅛ teaspoon
Salt   1 tablespoon
Pepper   to taste

In 2 quarts water, soak beans overnight or quick-soak. Add meats and bring to a boil, then cover and simmer 1 hour. Add barley, vegetables, and ginger and continue cooking until all ingredients are tender. Add salt and pepper. Remove meat and serve as an accompaniment to soup or reserve it for another meal; the soup itself is hearty enough for a meal. Serves 8.

Sopa Valencia

Large potatoes 2, peeled and sliced
Cabbage ½ small head, sliced
Onion 1 tablespoon chopped
Olive oil 3 tablespoons
Tomatoes 8-ounce can
Raw ham 4 ounces
Salt and pepper to taste
Stock 6 cups
Navy beans 1 cup cooked
Parsley 1 tablespoon chopped
Rice 3 tablespoons

Fry potatoes, cabbage, and onion in hot oil until cabbage is wilted. Add tomatoes, ham, salt and pepper, and stock; boil gently for 30 minutes. Add beans, parsley, and rice; cook until rice is tender. Serves 6 to 8.

Bean Soup

Pinto, navy, or marrow beans 1½ cups, cooked, liquid reserved
Beef broth 2 quarts
Garlic cloves 2, minced
Tomatoes 20-ounce can
Onion 1 cup finely chopped
Fresh thyme 1 sprig
Crumbled bacon, chopped parsley, yogurt, or sour cream topping

Combine beans, bean liquid, and next 5 ingredients and simmer 30 minutes. Top with bacon, parsley, or a dollop of yogurt or sour cream. Serves 4 to 6.

Pimiento–Soy Bisque

Soybeans   3 cups cooked
Pimientos   2, finely chopped
Milk   2 cups
Nonfat dry milk powder   ½ cup
Stock   1½ cups
Chervil   ½ teaspoon
Brewer's yeast   ¼ cup
Pimientos   2, finely chopped
Paprika

In blender, puree soybeans. Add next 6 ingredients and blend thoroughly. Add remaining 2 pimientos, pour mixture into saucepan and heat thoroughly. Sprinkle with paprika and serve. Serves 3 to 4.
Variation: Substitute other beans for soybeans.

Hot Persian Yogurt Soup

Brown rice   1 cup
Yellow split peas   ¼ cup
Water   5 cups
Salt   to taste
Spinach   ⅔ cup chopped
Water
Medium onion   1, chopped
Oil   2 tablespoons
Turmeric   2 teaspoons
Pepper   ½ teaspoon
Plain yogurt   3 cups

Put rice, split peas, and water in a pot. Bring to a boil, then simmer over low heat about 2 hours until peas are soft. Add salt and spinach and simmer until spinach is cooked. Add water to make mixture a little thicker than cake batter. Sauté onion in oil until tender. Add turmeric and pepper and stir mixture into peas and rice. Add yogurt and simmer 10 minutes to blend flavors. Serves 6.

Split Pea Soup with Pork

Water 6 cups
Split peas 12 ounces
Carrots 3, cut into 1-inch pieces
Medium onion 1, chopped
Marjoram leaves ½ teaspoon
Ground cloves ⅛ teaspoon
Salt 1 teaspoon
Pork 1 pound boneless

Put water in a Dutch oven or 4-quart kettle with peas and soak overnight or quick-soak. Add carrots, onion, marjoram, cloves, and salt. Simmer 30 minutes, or until peas are tender. Add pork and simmer 1½ hours more, or until pork has lost its pinkness. Remove pork from soup and cut into ½-inch cubes. Cool soup, then pour into blender a little at a time and puree. Reheat soup, pour into a tureen, and stir in pork cubes. Serve at once. Serves 6.

Curried Split Pea Soup

Yellow split peas 1 cup
Water 5 cups
Bacon strips 4, chopped
Medium onion 1, chopped
Garlic clove 1, minced
Celery 1 cup sliced
Carrots 1 cup sliced
Tomatoes 16-ounce can, chopped
Curry powder 1 teaspoon
Salt and pepper to taste
Parsley 2 tablespoons chopped

Combine first 5 ingredients in a large kettle. Cover and simmer gently until peas are tender. Add celery, carrots, tomatoes, and curry powder. Cover and continue to simmer until vegetables are tender. Add salt and pepper; sprinkle with parsley. Serves 4 to 6.

Scandinavian Yellow Pea Soup

Yellow split peas   1 pound
Water   3 quarts
Lean bacon or salt pork   1 pound, in 1 piece
Celery   1 large stalk, cut into 1-inch pieces
Leeks with tops   3, cut into 1-inch pieces
Medium carrots   3, peeled and cut into 1-inch pieces
Medium potatoes   3, peeled, and cut into 1-inch pieces
Medium onions   3, thinly sliced
Canadian bacon   1 pound
Ground thyme   ⅛ teaspoon
Vienna sausages   24-ounce can, drained

Soak peas overnight or quick-soak; drain. Put peas and water in a large kettle and slowly bring to a boil. Cover and cook over medium heat for 1 hour; skim off pea skins as they float to the top. Add bacon, cover, and simmer over very low heat about 2 hours, stirring occasionally, until peas are very soft. Add next 5 ingredients and simmer 30 minutes. Add Canadian bacon and thyme and simmer 30 minutes more; add sausages and continue to simmer for 15 minutes. If necessary, add a little hot water to bring soup to desired consistency. Remove bacon and Canadian bacon, slice, and serve with sausages on a heated platter as an accompaniment to soup. Serves 6 to 8.

Split Pea and Spinach Soup

Onion   2 cups chopped
Oil   2 tablespoons
Split peas   1 pound
Water   2 quarts
Bay leaves   2, crumbled
Basil   1 teaspoon
Frozen chopped spinach   10-ounce package, thawed
Salt   2 teaspoons
Pepper   ½ teaspoon
Ground cloves   ⅛ teaspoon
Parmesan cheese   ¼ cup grated

In a Dutch oven sauté onions in oil until golden. Add peas, water, bay leaves, and basil; cover and simmer about 1 hour until peas are tender. Add spinach, cover, and simmer 8 minutes more, stirring occasionally. Add salt, pepper, and cloves. Sprinkle with Parmesan and serve. Serves 4.

Punjab Pea Soup

Oil 1 tablespoon
Medium onion 1, thinly sliced
Curry powder 1½ teaspoons
Water 5 cups
Medium carrots 2, sliced
Celery 2 stalks, sliced
Split peas 1 cup
Garlic clove 1, minced
Chicken bouillon cubes 3
Bay leaf 1
Sugar 1 teaspoon
Thyme leaves ⅛ teaspoon
Dried rosemary ⅛ teaspoon
Pepper ¼ teaspoon
Salt to taste

In a 3-quart pan, heat oil over medium heat; add onion and curry powder and cook until onion is limp. Add remaining ingredients except salt and simmer 1 hour, stirring occasionally. Remove bay leaf; puree soup in a blender or food processor. Add salt and serve. Serves 4 to 6.

Bazillah Soup

Dried peas 1 cup
Water 3 cups
Meat stock or bouillon 1 cup
Onion 1, chopped
Parsley 1 teaspoon chopped
Oil 2 tablespoons
Soy flour 1 tablespoon
Salt and pepper to taste
Yogurt 1 cup

Soak peas overnight or quick-soak; drain. In a large pot, combine peas with water, stock, onion, and parsley and simmer until peas are tender. Blend oil and flour into a smooth paste and add to peas, stirring until well mixed. Add salt and pepper and simmer 20 minutes more, stirring occasionally. Just before serving, add yogurt and stir well; serve hot. Serves 4 to 6.

White Bean Minestrone

Small white beans 1 cup
Water 2½ cups
Chicken or Minestrone Stock 1 cup
Pearl or long grain rice ½ cup
Large tomatoes 2, chopped
Carrots 4, sliced
Green beans ½ cup cut into 1- to 2-inch pieces
Celery 4 stalks, sliced
Parsley 1 cup chopped
Ham reserved from Minestrone Stock (optional)
Parmesan cheese topping
Pesto Sauce topping

Put beans and water in a saucepan and bring to a boil, then remove from heat and allow to set at least 1 hour or overnight. In a large saucepan, bring stock to a boil and add beans and their soaking water. Simmer, covered, about 1½ hours until beans are very tender. Add rice, tomatoes, and carrots and simmer, covered, for 10 minutes. Add green beans, celery, and parsley and simmer, uncovered, 5 minutes more. Add ham. Serve in warmed bowls; top each serving with Parmesan cheese and 1 to 2 teaspoons Pesto Sauce. Makes 4 quarts.

Minestrone Stock

Chicken wings or backs 1 to 2 pounds
Ham hocks 2 pounds, cut into 1- to 2-inch slices
Large onions 2, quartered
Large carrots 2, cut into 2-inch slices
Parsley 10 sprigs
Water 6 cups
Chicken broth 6 cups

Combine all ingredients in a pot. Cover, bring to a boil, and simmer 3 hours. Cool, then drain off broth. Reserve ham meat and discard the rest. Cover stock and chill; skim fat off top and discard. Makes 11 cups.
Note: This freezes well.

Pesto Sauce

Fresh basil leaves 1 cup (packed)
Parmesan cheese ½ cup grated
Olive oil ¼ cup

Put ingredients in a blender and puree to a coarse consistency. Use immediately or refrigerate. Makes ⅔ cup.

Old-Fashioned Minestrone

Large onion 1, chopped
Large carrots 2, chopped
Celery 3 stalks, chopped
Medium potatoes 2, peeled and chopped
Green beans 8 ounces, cut into 1-inch pieces
Olive oil or salad oil ½ cup
Water 1 quart
Cabbage ½ small head, shredded
Spinach 5 ounces, coarsely shredded
Medium tomatoes 6, peeled
Medium zucchini 2, chopped
Beef bouillon cubes 4
Salt 1 teaspoon
White beans 2 cups cooked or
    Canned cannellini beans 16-ounce can, drained
Red kidney beans 2 cups cooked or
    Canned red kidney beans 16-ounce can, drained
Grated Parmesan cheese topping

In a Dutch oven cook first 5 ingredients in oil over medium heat about 20 minutes, stirring occasionally. Add next 7 ingredients, increase heat to high, and bring mixture to a boil. Break up tomatoes, then reduce heat, cover, and simmer 40 minutes, stirring occasionally. Stir in beans; cook about 15 minutes more to allow soup to thicken. Serve with grated cheese. Makes 4 quarts.

Summer Minestrone Soup

Chicken broth 2 quarts
Green beans 8 ounces, cut into 1-inch pieces
Celery 3 stalks, thinly sliced
Medium leeks 3, chopped
Medium zucchini 2, cut into bite-sized pieces
Large tomatoes 2, peeled and chopped
Salt 1 teaspoon
Pepper ¼ teaspoon
White beans 4 cups cooked or
    Canned cannellini beans two 16-ounce cans, drained
Fresh basil 2 tablespoons chopped or
    Dried basil 2 teaspoons
Garlic cloves 3, crushed
Olive oil or salad oil 2 teaspoons
Parmesan cheese 6 tablespoons grated

In a large saucepan, bring chicken broth to a boil over medium heat. Add next 7 ingredients and bring to a boil again. Reduce heat and cook 20 to 30 minutes, or until vegetables are tender. Add beans and basil and cook 10 minutes more. Blend garlic with oil and stir into soup. Serve immediately, topped with grated cheese. Serves 4.

Leafy Bean Soup

Medium onion   1, finely chopped
Garlic clove   1, minced
Butter or margarine   2 tablespoons
Regular strength chicken broth   two 14½-ounce cans
Bay leaf   1
Spinach   1 bunch (about 8 ounces)
White kidney beans or garbanzos   2 cups cooked, liquid drained
   and ½ cup reserved
Salt and pepper   to taste
Freshly grated Parmesan cheese

In a Dutch oven sauté onion and garlic in butter over medium heat until golden brown. Add broth and bay leaf; simmer 15 minutes. Wash spinach and discard stems. Stack the leaves and slice crosswise into ¼-inch strips. Add beans and reserved cooking liquid to broth. Bring soup back to simmer and cook for 1 minute. Add spinach and simmer 2 minutes more. Add salt and pepper. Serve with grated Parmesan. Serves 4 to 6.

Greek Bean Soup

Small white beans   1 pound
Water   2 quarts
Large onions   2, finely chopped
Garlic cloves   2, finely minced
Carrots   2, finely chopped
Celery with leaves   3 stalks, chopped
Parsley   ½ cup chopped
Olive oil   ½ to 1 cup
Salt and pepper   to taste

Soak beans overnight or quick-soak; drain. Put beans and water in a pot; bring to a boil. Add remaining ingredients except salt and pepper and simmer about 1½ to 2 hours until beans are tender. Add salt and pepper, and serve. Serves 4 to 5.

French Ham and Flageolets Stew

Flageolets 4 cups
Ham hocks 1½ pounds, cut into chunks
Onions 2, chopped
Parsley 3 cups chopped (lightly packed)
Sliced stewed tomatoes 16-ounce can
Regular strength chicken or beef broth 14½-ounce can
Water 6 cups
Salt and pepper to taste

Soak beans overnight or quick-soak; drain. Combine all ingredients except salt and pepper in a 5-quart Dutch oven and bring to a boil. Simmer, covered, until meat and beans are tender. Add salt and pepper. Ladle into deep plates or broad soup bowls. Serve with hot French bread. Serves 6 to 8.

Garbanzo Pot

Garbanzos 1 pound
Water 1 quart
Ham hocks 2
Bay leaf 1
Oregano ½ teaspoon
Sweet or hot Italian sausage 1 pound, cut into chunks
Large onion 1, chopped
Medium green pepper 1, seeded and chopped
Garlic clove 1, crushed
Worcestershire sauce ½ teaspoon
Salt ½ teaspoon
Pepper dash

Put garbanzos and water in a large kettle and soak overnight or quick-soak. Add ham hocks, bay leaf, and oregano. Bring to a boil, then cover and simmer 2 hours until garbanzos are tender but not mushy. Discard bay leaf. Sauté sausage until fat has appeared in the pan, then add onion, green pepper, and garlic and sauté until vegetables are lightly browned. Add to garbanzos with remaining ingredients; cover and simmer about 20 minutes until sausage is done. Adjust seasonings to taste. Serves 6.

Cuban Cocido

Garbanzos 2 cups
Water
Beef or veal 2 pounds
Pork 1 pound
Bacon strips 6
Dried beef jerky 8 ounces
Salt pork 8 ounces
Pork sausage links 1 pound
Salt to taste
Plantains or firm bananas 2, unpeeled and cut into 1-inch chunks
Fresh or frozen corn 2 ears, husked and cut into 3 or 4 pieces
Summer squash 1 pound, pared and quartered
Medium carrots 4, peeled and sliced
Small eggplant 1, peeled and chopped
Cabbage ½ head, chopped
Fresh green beans 2 cups, cut into 1-inch pieces
Potatoes 6, chopped
Onions 2, quartered
Small white turnip 1, peeled and chopped
Tomatoes 4, quartered
Garlic cloves 3, crushed
Chili powder pinch
Ground cumin pinch
Ground coriander pinch
Saffron ½ teaspoon

Soak garbanzos overnight or quick-soak; drain. Half-fill a 1½-gallon kettle with water and add next 7 ingredients and garbanzos. Cover, and cook slowly over moderate heat for 90 minutes; add next 11 ingredients. Mix garlic, chili powder, cumin, and coriander with a little soup to make a paste; stir into soup. Cook about 45 minutes until all vegetables are soft. Just before serving, dissolve saffron in a little of the liquid and add to soup, stirring to blend. Cut up the meats and serve with vegetables in hot soup bowls with a little of the broth. Serves 10 to 12.

Puchero de Sonora (Sonora Stew)

Garbanzos 8 ounces
Water
Lean stew meat 1 pound, cut into small pieces
Salt to taste
Large onion 1, chopped
Whole string beans 8 ounces
Shortening 3 tablespoons
Garlic clove 1, minced
Chili powder 1 tablespoon
Tomato sauce 1 cup

Soak garbanzos overnight or quick-soak; drain. Cook in a generous amount of water; when almost tender, remove garbanzos from water and remove the skins. Return garbanzos to water; add stew meat, salt, and onion. Continue to cook until meat is almost tender, then tie string beans into 6 bundles and add to stew. Melt shortening in a small pan. Add garlic and cook until it is transparent. Add chili powder and tomato sauce; cook 5 minutes more and add to stew. Cook until meat and vegetables are very tender. Serves 4 to 6.

Kidney Bean and Lamb Stew

Kidney beans 1 pound
Water 3 cups
Large lamb shank 1
Butter 2 tablespoons
Onion 1 cup chopped
Celery 1 cup chopped
Carrots ½ cup chopped
Garlic clove 1, minced
Tomato juice 1 cup
Salt 3 teaspoons
Pepper ¼ teaspoon
Bay leaf 1
Ground cloves ¼ teaspoon
Thyme ¼ teaspoon crushed
Lemon juice 2 teaspoons

Combine beans and water and soak overnight or quick-soak. Drain, reserving liquid; add enough water to liquid to make 6 cups. Brown lamb shank in butter in a Dutch oven. Add vegetables and sauté until tender but firm. Add beans, liquid, and remaining ingredients except lemon juice. Bring to a boil; reduce heat, cover, and simmer 2 hours. Remove bay leaf and discard. Remove lamb; cool slightly, then remove meat from bone. Cut meat into small pieces and return to soup; discard bone. Add lemon juice to soup, heat thoroughly, and serve. Serves 6.

Spicy Sausage and Lentil Stew

Lentils 1 pound
Water 5 cups
Small bay leaf 1
Salt 1 teaspoon
Garlic salt ⅛ teaspoon
Dry mustard ⅛ teaspoon
Cinnamon ⅛ teaspoon
Ground cloves ⅛ teaspoon
Ginger ⅛ teaspoon
Nutmeg ⅛ teaspoon
Dried savory ⅛ teaspoon
Dried thyme ⅛ teaspoon
Pepper ⅛ teaspoon
Polish or German sausage 8 ounces, cut into ½-inch slices
Medium onions 2, cut into wedges
Tomato juice 2 cups
Tomato sauce 2 cups
Molasses 3 tablespoons
Bottled barbecue sauce 2 tablespoons

Combine first 13 ingredients in a Dutch oven. Bring to a boil, then reduce heat, cover, and simmer 40 minutes. Cook sausage and onions in a skillet until meat is done and onion is golden brown; add to lentils along with remaining ingredients. Cover and simmer 15 minutes more. Remove bay leaf, and serve. Serves 8 to 10.

Burgundy Meat and Bean Stew

Pinto beans   2½ cups
Water
Meaty beef bones*   1 pound
Meaty ham bone*   ¾ pound
Garlic clove   1, minced
Salt   1 teaspoon
Pepper   ¼ teaspoon
Bay leaf   1
Tomatoes   16-ounce can, cut up
Burgundy wine   1½ cups
Tomato sauce   8-ounce can
Brown sugar   2 tablespoons

In a Dutch oven, cover beans with water and soak overnight or quick-soak; do not drain. Add next 6 ingredients; cover and simmer 1½ hours, stirring occasionally. Remove bones; cool, then cut off the meat and return meat to pot. Add undrained tomatoes and remaining ingredients. Cover and simmer about 45 minutes until beans are tender. Remove bay leaf. Mash beans slightly, adjust seasonings to taste, and serve. Serves 10.
* Leftover beef and ham may be used instead of bones.

Soybean–Vegetable Stew

Water   6 cups
Celery   1 bunch, chopped
Large celery root   1, chopped
Carrots   4, chopped
Rutabaga   1, chopped
Turnip   1, chopped
Parsley   3 or 4 sprigs, chopped
Medium onion   1, chopped
Soybeans   1½ cups cooked
Tomatoes   16-ounce can, drained
Cut green beans   8-ounce can, drained
Soy sauce   1 tablespoon or
    Seasoning of choice   to taste
Brewer's yeast   to taste (optional)

Bring water to a boil in a large pot. Add next 10 ingredients, cover, and simmer until vegetables are tender. Add soy sauce and yeast. Serves 6 to 8.

White Bean Pottage

White beans   8 ounces
Water
Salt   to taste
Lean pork   1 pound, cut into cubes
Oil   2 tablespoons
Medium onion   1, chopped
Sweet pepper   ½, seeded and chopped
Ham   1 slice, chopped
Chorizos or pork sausages   2, skinned and chopped
Tomato sauce   8-ounce can
Cabbage   one ¼-inch wedge

Cover beans with water and soak overnight or quick-soak; do not drain. Cook for 2 hours; add salt and pork. Heat oil in a large pot and sauté onion, pepper, ham, and chorizos. Add tomato sauce and bring to a boil. Pour beans with liquid and meat mixture into the pot and add cabbage. Simmer about 2 hours until pottage thickens. Serves 6 to 8.

Oven Pork Stew with Baked Beans

Lean pork butt   3½ pounds boned
Oil   2 tablespoons
Large onions   2, chopped
Baked beans   4 cups or
    Canned baked beans   two 16-ounce cans or
    Canned pork and beans   30-ounce can
Prepared mustard   3 tablespoons
Brown sugar   2 tablespoons

Trim fat from pork and cut the meat into 1-inch cubes. Place oil in a shallow pan; set the oven at 500° and place the pan in the oven while it heats. Add meat and onions to the pan and cook, uncovered, about 15 minutes until meat is browned, stirring often. Combine remaining ingredients; reduce oven heat to 350°, pour the bean mixture over the meat, and bake 30 minutes, or until meat is tender. Skim off fat and serve. Serves 6.

Baked-Bean Stew

Ground beef   8 ounces
Garlic salt   1 teaspoon
Baked beans   4 cups or
    Canned baked beans   two 16-ounce cans
Corn   1 cup cooked or
    Canned corn   8-ounce can, drained
Tomatoes   8¼-ounce can, cut up

In a saucepan, brown beef with garlic salt, stirring to separate beef. Add remaining ingredients and heat through, stirring occasionally. Serves 6.

Side Dishes

Spanish Beans with Sour Cream

Black beans   1 pound
Water   3 to 4 cups
Large onion   1, finely chopped
Carrot   1, finely chopped
Green pepper   1, seeded and finely chopped
Salt   ½ teaspoon
Pepper   ½ teaspoon
Rum   ¼ cup
Butter   3 tablespoons
Sour cream   2 cups
Green onions   ½ cup thinly sliced

Combine beans and water in a Dutch oven; soak overnight or quick-soak; do not drain. Add onion, carrot, and green pepper and simmer gently 2½ to 3 hours, adding more water as needed to keep beans moist. When beans are tender but not mushy, add salt, pepper, rum, and butter; stir until butter melts. Turn into a serving dish and garnish with a mound of sour cream sprinkled with green onions. Pass remaining sour cream and green onions at the table. Serves 8 to 10.

Feijao Preto Simples

Black beans   1 pound
Water
Bacon drippings   1 tablespoon
Onion   1, grated
Garlic clove   1, minced
Salt   1 teaspoon
Pepper

Soak beans overnight or quick-soak; drain. Cover beans with water and simmer 1 to 3 hours until beans are tender. Melt bacon drippings in a skillet. Add onion and garlic and sauté until golden. Add 1 cup of beans in their liquid, mashing beans thoroughly. Add more liquid if needed and bring to a boil. Season with salt and pepper. Add onion-bean mixture to remaining beans and simmer 30 minutes. Adjust seasonings to taste and cook until mixture thickens to the consistency of a medium sauce. Serves 8 to 10.

Cuban Black Beans

Large black beans 1 pound
Water 5 cups
Garlic clove 1, cut in half
Salt 1 teaspoon
Oil 2 tablespoons
Garlic cloves 3, minced
Powdered sage ¼ teaspoon
Bay leaf 1
Green pepper 1, seeded and chopped
Onion 1, chopped
Cider vinegar 1 tablespoon
Salt and pepper to taste

Soak beans overnight or quick-soak; drain. Pour beans into a 2-quart pot and cover with 5 cups water, or enough to cover beans by 1½ inches. Add garlic, cover, and cook slowly for 2 hours. Add salt and cook until beans are tender; drain. Heat oil in saucepan; add next 5 ingredients and simmer until vegetables are tender. Add vinegar, salt, and pepper and cook, stirring constantly, until sauce has thickened. Remove bay leaf and discard. Pour sauce over beans and adjust seasonings to taste. Serves 6.

Havana Black Beans

Black beans 1 pound
Water 1 quart
Salt pork 5 ounces, chopped
Garlic cloves 3, minced
Medium onion 1, chopped
Medium green pepper 1, seeded and chopped
Celery ½ cup finely chopped
Honey ¼ cup
Prepared mustard ¼ cup
Paprika 2 teaspoons
Chili powder 1 teaspoon
Oregano 1 teaspoon
Pepper ¼ teaspoon
Salt to taste
White rice 8 to 10 servings
Lemon wedges garnish
Sliced green onions garnish

Combine beans and water in a Dutch oven and soak overnight or quick-soak. Add salt pork to undrained beans. Add next 10 ingredients and stir to blend. Cover and simmer gently for 3 hours, or until beans are tender, adding more water as needed. Add salt. Serve over white rice, garnished with lemon wedges and green onions. Serves 8 to 10.
Note: This dish traditionally is served with pork and fried bananas.

Black Bean Cake

Black beans 2 cups cooked, slightly juicy
Bread crumbs 1¼ cups
Tomato sauce ½ cup
Onion ¼ cup chopped
Egg 1, slightly beaten
Salt and pepper to taste
Hard-cooked egg wedges garnish
Crisp bacon slices garnish
Tomato sauce

Combine beans and bread crumbs. Add tomato sauce, onion, and egg; season. Turn into a well-buttered 1½-quart pudding mold and bake at 375° approximately 45 minutes. Unmold and garnish with egg wedges and bacon slices. Serve with tomato sauce. Serves 4 to 6.

Texas Black-eyed Peas

Black-eyed peas 1 pound
Water
Presoaked soy grits ½ cup
Brewer's yeast 3 tablespoons (optional)
Chili sauce 1 cup
Chili powder 1 tablespoon
Dark molasses ½ cup
Onion 1, chopped
Salt and pepper to taste

Cover peas with water; soak overnight or quick-soak. Simmer until peas are tender but not mushy. Combine remaining ingredients and add to peas. Place in a greased casserole, cover, and bake at 350° for 45 minutes, adding more water if needed. Remove cover for last 15 minutes. Serves 6.

Crispy Fried Beans

Shortening   3 tablespoons
Onion   1 teaspoon chopped
Mexican brown beans   8 ounces, cooked and mashed
Salt   to taste
Shredded cheese   topping
Totopos

Melt shortening; add onion and cook until transparent. Add beans and salt and cook, mashing with a fork or masher and stirring steadily, until the mixture is dry. Form into a roll (roll should be dry but crispy and rich brown on the outside). Top with cheese and serve with totopos (squares of fried tortillas). Serves 6.

Creamy Beans

Bacon drippings   2 tablespoons
Onion   1 teaspoon chopped
Flour   1 teaspoon
Mexican brown beans   8 ounces, cooked, liquid reserved*
Salt   to taste
**Chopped green pepper,
    chili powder, or sliced sausage**   garnish (optional)

Melt drippings in frying pan; add onion and cook until transparent. Add flour and cook until mixture becomes light brown. Add to beans and reserved liquid; season to taste. Cook until creamy in texture. Garnish with green pepper, chili powder, or sausage if desired. Serves 6 to 8.
* Red kidney beans may be substituted for Mexican brown beans.

Frijoles Mexicanas

Mexican brown beans   8 ounces*
Water
Lard   1 tablespoon
Onion   1, finely chopped
Salt   to taste

Soak beans overnight or quick-soak; drain. Place beans in a large kettle with generous amount of water, lard, onion, and salt. Cover and cook, adding warm water as needed, until beans are very tender. Serves 6 to 8.
* Kidney beans may be substituted for Mexican brown beans.

Little Flutes

Flageolets   4 cups
Water or stock ˏ 6 cups
Butter   1 to 2 tablespoons
Salt and pepper   to taste

Soak beans overnight or quick-soak; drain. Combine beans and water or stock; bring to a boil. Simmer about 1½ to 2 hours until beans are tender but retain shape (beans should be easy to mash). Add more water as needed to keep beans moist. Butter and season to taste; serve as a side dish. Serves 4 to 6.

Garbanzos Guarnición

Green peppers   2, seeded and chopped
Onions   2, coarsely chopped
Olive oil   2 tablespoons
Tomato puree   ½ cup
Garbanzos   1 cup, cooked

Sauté green peppers and onions in oil for 3 minutes. Add tomato puree and garbanzos and simmer about 30 minutes until garbanzos are tender. Serves 4.

Braised Garbanzos

Garbanzos   4 cups cooked, liquid reserved, or
    Canned garbanzos   two 16-ounce cans
Onions   4, finely chopped
Garlic cloves   2, finely minced
Salt and pepper   to taste
Tomatoes with juice   2 cups chopped
Parsley   ½ cup chopped
Mint   ¼ cup chopped (optional)

Place garbanzos with liquid in a heavy pot or Dutch oven; bring to a boil. Add remaining ingredients and cook over low heat for 20 minutes, keeping the mixture at a low boiling point. Serves 6.
Variation: The Spanish add slices of garlic sausage.

Spanish Cabbage

Garbanzos   8 ounces
Water
Cabbage   1 medium head, chopped
Shortening   3 tablespoons
Onion   1 teaspoon chopped
Garlic clove   1, minced
Ham   4 ounces, chopped
Tomatoes   2 cups chopped
Salt and pepper   to taste
Pimientos   2, cut into strips

Soak garbanzos overnight or quick-soak; drain. Boil garbanzos in water until skins can be easily removed. Return skinned peas to kettle and cook until tender. In another pot, cook cabbage for 10 minutes; add to garbanzos. Melt shortening and sauté onion and garlic until soft. Add ham and tomatoes and cook 5 minutes. Season well with salt and pepper; add to garbanzos. Cook a few minutes more to blend flavors. Serve hot, garnished with pimiento strips. Serves 6 to 8.

Beans and Cabbage

Large onion   1, chopped
Olive oil   2 tablespoons
Garbanzos   2 cups, cooked, liquid reserved, or
    Canned garbanzos   two 15-ounce cans
Cabbage   one 4-pound head, shredded
Salt and pepper   to taste

Cook onion in oil until golden. Add beans with liquid and the cabbage; season. Cover and cook about 15 minutes until cabbage is done. Serves 6.

Beans in Wine Sauce

Celery or bok choy 3 stalks, cut into 1-inch pieces
Garlic cloves 2 or 3, finely minced
Oil or margarine 2 to 3 tablespoons
Beef or vegetable bouillon 1 cube
Bay leaf 1, broken
Thyme 1 teaspoon
Rosemary 1 teaspoon
Salt and pepper to taste
Kidney beans 2 to 3 pounds, cooked, or
   Canned kidney beans three 16-ounce cans, drained
Onion 1, finely chopped
Parsley ½ cup chopped
Flour 2 tablespoons
Red wine 1 cup or
   Bean liquid ¾ cup and
   Vinegar ¼ cup

Sauté celery and garlic in oil. When soft, add next 5 ingredients and stir until bouillon is dissolved. Add beans, onion, and parsley, stirring well. Sprinkle with flour and stir to coat beans. Add wine; mix well. Simmer about 5 minutes to thicken sauce. Serves 6 to 8.

Kidney Beans in Brown Butter Sauce

Butter 2 tablespoons
Flour 2 tablespoons
Boiling water 1 cup
Salt ½ teaspoon
Pepper dash
Kidney beans 2 cups cooked

In a small saucepan, cook butter over high heat until golden brown. Stir in flour and cook until mixture bubbles and flour turns golden. Remove from heat and beat in boiling water until smooth and thick; add salt and pepper. Heat beans in the sauce and serve as a meat substitute. Serves **4**.

Eurasian Lentils

Oil   3 tablespoons
Garlic clove   1, minced
Onion   1, grated
Soy flour   3 tablespoons
Brewer's yeast   3 tablespoons
Lentils   4 cups cooked and pureed
Honey   1 tablespoon
Tarragon leaves   1 teaspoon
Cheddar or Parmesan cheese   ½ cup shredded

Heat oil and sauté garlic and onion until golden brown. Add remaining ingredients except cheese; cover and simmer until thoroughly heated. Top with cheese and serve. Serves 6.

Lentils with Fruit

Lentils   1 pound
Water
Shortening   2 tablespoons
Fresh or canned tomatoes   3, chopped
Garlic clove   1, minced
Onion   1 tablespoon chopped
Fresh or canned pineapple   2 slices, each cut into 4 to 6 pieces
Sweet potato   1, boiled, peeled, and cut into ½-inch slices
Apple   1, sliced
Bananas   2, sliced
Salt and pepper   to taste

Boil lentils in generous amount of water until tender; drain. Melt shortening and add tomatoes, garlic, and onion; cook about 5 minutess until blended. Add pineapple, sweet potato, apple, and bananas, and cook until apple is tender and mixture is creamy. Add lentils, and season to taste. Serves 4 to 6.

Linzen Fleishig

Water 2 cups
Lentils or split peas 1 cup
Beef or veal stock 1 quart
Salt and pepper to taste

In 2 cups water, soak lentils overnight or quick-soak; do not drain. Add stock and bring to a boil, then simmer until lentils are very soft. Puree and season to taste. Serves 5 to 6.

Romanian Slaitta

Lima or navy beans 8 ounces, cooked, liquid drained
and ¼ cup reserved
Garlic clove 1, finely minced
Salt to taste
Large onions 3, cut into ¼-inch slices and separated into rings
Butter

Mash beans thoroughly and add reserved liquid, garlic, and salt. Place on a platter. Sauté onions in butter until golden and spread over beans. Serve as a side dish with sliced meats. Serves 5 to 6.

Navy Beans and Pearl Barley

Navy beans 1 pound
Pearl barley ½ cup
Water
Small ham butt 1
Garlic clove 1, minced
Small onion 1, chopped
Bay leaf 1
Salt and pepper to taste

Soak beans overnight or quick-soak; drain. Put beans and barley in a large kettle and cover with water. Add remaining ingredients except salt and pepper; simmer 2 hours. Add salt and pepper and simmer 3 hours more. Remove bay leaf and adjust salt to taste. Serves 8.

Refried Beans

Pinto beans   1 pound
Water   7 cups
Onion   1 cup coarsely chopped
Garlic clove   1, minced
Salt   1 tablespoon
Bacon drippings   ½ cup

Combine beans and water in a large saucepan; soak overnight or quick-soak. Add onion and garlic and return to a boil. Reduce heat, cover, and simmer until beans are very tender. Add salt, then mash beans with a potato masher. In a large skillet, heat bacon drippings over low heat. Add beans and cook, stirring constantly, until drippings are absorbed and beans are hot. Makes about 7 cups.

Refried Beans with Cheese

Pinto beans   1 pound
Water   5 cups
Monterey Jack cheese   1 pound
Crushed dried chili peppers   to taste
Salt   to taste
Butter   1 cup
Lard   1 cup

Soak beans overnight or quick-soak; drain. Combine beans and water and simmer until beans are tender; drain. Chop beans and cheese using the medium-sized blade of a food chopper or process lightly, and mash. Add peppers and salt. Melt butter and lard in a large frying pan. Add bean mixture and cook, stirring constantly, over medium heat for 30 minutes. Serve with meat and tortillas. Serves 6 to 8.

Roman Beans with Oil

Roman or cranberry beans   1 pound
Olive oil   ¼ cup
Garlic   1 tablespoon finely minced
Water   6 cups
Sage leaves   2 to 4
Salt and pepper   to taste
Olive oil

Soak beans overnight or quick-soak; drain. Heat oil in a Dutch oven; add garlic and cook until golden. Add beans, water, sage, salt, and pepper. Cook uncovered about 1 hour. Serve in its liquid as a side dish, with olive oil sprinkled over each serving. Serves 6 to 8.

Eggs with Green Sauce

Eggs 6, hard-cooked
Onion 1 tablespoon chopped
Parsley 1 tablespoon chopped
Green olives 3 tablespoons chopped
Capers 1 tablespoon chopped
Salt and pepper to taste
Butter 1 tablespoon
Green pea soup 2 cups pureed
Butter 1 tablespoon
Chopped parsley garnish

Cut eggs in half lengthwise and remove yolks. Mash yolks and mix with onion, parsley, olives, and capers. Season with salt and pepper. Melt 1 tablespoon butter over low heat and add yolk mixture. When mixture becomes very thick, cool slightly, then fill the egg whites with mounds of this mixture. Place the filled eggs on a hot, deep platter. Heat pea soup with butter. Cover the egg halves with soup. Sprinkle with parsley before serving. Serves 6.

Linguisa Beans

White beans 2 cups
Water 6 cups
Ham hock 1
Large onion 1, sliced
Tomatoes 8-ounce can
Tomato sauce 8-ounce can
Tomato paste 6-ounce can
Garlic clove 1, minced
Bay leaves 2
Linguisa or chorizo 1 pound, cut into ½-inch pieces

Soak beans overnight or quick-soak; drain. Cook beans in water until tender; add ham hock and onion. Bring to a boil, then simmer 2 hours. Add remaining ingredients and simmer gently 3 to 4 hours more until beans are very tender. Remove bay leaves and serve. Serves 8 to 10.

Main Dishes

Frijoles Carmelita

Onion 1 tablespoon chopped
Sweet pepper 1, seeded and chopped
Garlic clove 1, minced
Oil
Beans 2 cups cooked
Chicken 2 cups cooked, boned, and chopped
Tomatoes 16-ounce can
Chili powder 2 teaspoons (optional)
Salt to taste

Sauté onion, pepper, and garlic in oil until onion is golden. Add remaining ingredients and simmer 1½ hours, stirring often. Serves 6.

Black Bean Tutu

Black beans 3 cups cooked, liquid reserved
Manioc Meal or Cream of Wheat
Vinegar 2 tablespoons
Bacon ¼ cup chopped
Smoked sausage 8 ounces, thinly sliced
Onion 1, thinly sliced
Cooked spinach or kale garnish
Hard-cooked egg slices garnish

Heat beans in their liquid and add meal to attain the consistency of mush. Stir well and remove from heat; add vinegar. Spoon into a serving dish. Fry bacon and sausage together and drain well; place on top of beans. Fry onion in bacon drippings and spread over bacon and sausage. Surround with cooked spinach and egg slices before serving. Serves 4.

Brazilian Feijoada

Black beans   3 cups
Water
Salt   1 teaspoon
Beef brisket   2 pounds, cut into large cubes
Beef tongue   2 pounds, peeled and cut into cubes
Dried spicy sausage   8 ounces
Lean salt pork   1 pound, chopped
Bay leaf   1
Garlic cloves   3, minced
Butter   1 tablespoon
Oranges   2, peeled and sliced

Soak beans overnight or quick-soak; drain. In a large kettle, cover beans with water. Bring to a boil; add next 6 ingredients. Cover and simmer over low heat about 2 hours until beans are tender. Remove bay leaf and discard. Brown garlic in butter. Mash 1 cup of cooked beans with garlic and butter, blending well. Return to cooking meats and stir well. Adjust seasoning to taste. Serve on a large platter with sliced meats surrounding the beans; garnish with orange slices. Serves 6 to 8.
Note: Feijoada traditionally is served with collard or mustard greens.

Black Beans

Onions   2, chopped
Green pepper   1, seeded and chopped
Garlic clove   1, minced
Oil   1 tablespoon
Black beans   2 cups cooked
Bay leaves   2
Sea salt   1 teaspoon
Marjoram   ¼ teaspoon
Garlic clove   1, minced
Hot cooked rice

In a saucepan, sauté onions, pepper, and garlic clove in oil. Add beans; partially mash them. Add bay leaves, salt, and marjoram. Cover and simmer 15 minutes. Add garlic and simmer 5 minutes more. Remove bay leaves and serve beans over rice. Serves 4.

Black Rice

Black beans ¼ cup
Large onion 1, chopped
Water
Oil 2 tablespoons
Salt to taste
Rice 8 ounces
Hot water
Oil 3 tablespoons
Garlic clove 1
Small onion 1, chopped
Tomato paste 3 tablespoons
Bean liquid 5 cups
Salt to taste
Parsley 1 sprig
Ham ½ cup boiled and chopped
Peas ½ cup cooked or
    Canned peas 4-ounce can
Artichoke hearts 6, cooked (optional)
Shredded cheese

Soak beans overnight or quick-soak; drain. Cook beans and onion in generous amount of water with 2 tablespoons oil until beans are tender. Add salt. Drain, reserving 5 cups of liquid. Using a blender, food processor, or sieve, puree beans and onion with reserved liquid (puree will be very thin). Soak rice in hot water for 15 minutes; drain. Fry in hot oil with garlic and chopped onion. When rice is golden, add tomato paste and cook about 2 minutes more. Put bean puree in a large pot and add rice mixture, salt, and parsley. Cook over low heat until rice is barely tender. Add ham, peas, and artichoke hearts. Cook until rice is tender. Top with cheese. Serves 10 to 12.

Black-eyed Supper

Butter 2 tablespoons
Flour 2 tablespoons
Curry powder 1½ teaspoons
Salt ½ teaspoon
Milk ¾ cup
Sharp Cheddar cheese ¾ cup shredded
Black-eyed peas 5 to 6 cups cooked or
    Canned black-eyed peas three 16-ounce cans, drained
Frankfurters 6, split lengthwise

Melt butter in medium saucepan. Stir in flour, curry powder, and salt; cook, stirring constantly, for 1 minute. Stir in milk and continue to cook and stir until sauce is thick and bubbly. Remove from heat; add cheese and stir until cheese melts. Add peas, spoon into 1½-quart casserole, and top with frankfurters. Bake at 350° for 30 minutes, or until bubbly. Serves 6.

French-Style Lamb and Flageolets

Flageolets 4 cups
Leg of lamb 6½ to 7 pounds
Salt and pepper to taste
Water or stock 6 cups
Butter ½ cup, softened
Flour 1 tablespoon
Lemon peel 1 teaspoon grated
Parsley ¼ cup chopped

Soak beans overnight or quick-soak; drain. Sprinkle leg of lamb with salt and pepper and place skin-side down on a rack in a roasting pan. Roast at 300°, allowing 30 minutes per pound for medium and 35 minutes per pound for well-done roast (meat thermometer should register between 175° and 180°). Combine beans and water or stock; bring to a boil. Simmer about 1½ to 2 hours until beans are tender but retain shape. Blend butter and flour and add enough bean liquid to make a medium-thick paste. Add lemon peel and parsley; stir gently into beans. Put leg of lamb on a platter and spoon beans around lamb. Serves 6.

Garbanzo Patties

Garbanzos 1 cup cooked
Water ½ cup
Rice 1 cup cooked
Brewer's yeast 2 tablespoons
Brazil nuts 3 tablespoons chopped
Onion powder ⅓ teaspoon
Poultry seasoning ⅔ teaspoon
Salt ⅔ teaspoon
Garlic powder dash

Puree garbanzos and water and pour into a mixing bowl. Add remaining ingredients and mix well. Drop by tablespoonfuls onto a greased baking sheet and bake at 350° for 10 minutes. Turn patties over and cover; bake an additional 5 minutes. Serves 6.

Garbanzo–Bulgur Patties

Garbanzos 1 cup
Water ½ cup
Onion ½ cup chopped
Oil 2 tablespoons
Salt ½ teaspoon
Chicken bouillon cube 1
Boiling water 1 cup
Bulgur or cracked wheat ½ cup
Garlic powder ⅛ teaspoon
Parsley garnish

Soak garbanzos overnight or quick-soak; drain. Place garbanzos in a blender with water and blend until fine. Sauté onion in oil. Stir salt and bouillon cube into boiling water in a heavy saucepan until bouillon dissolves; add bulgur and stir until grain is evenly moistened. Reduce heat to low; add garlic powder and sautéed onions with oil. Add ground garbanzos, mixing thoroughly. Drop by tablespoonfuls onto a greased skillet or baking dish. Cover and bake at 350° for 10 minutes. Reduce heat to 300°; turn patties over, cover, and bake about 15 minutes more. Garnish with parsley and serve with favorite gravy or sauce. Serves 6.

Falafel

Garbanzos 8 ounces
Large garlic clove 1, cut in half
Large onion (about ⅓ pound) 1, thinly sliced
Ground cumin ½ teaspoon
Ground or fresh coriander ½ teaspoon (optional)
Parsley 6 sprigs
Salt and pepper to taste
Cayenne ⅛ teaspoon
Baking powder ¼ teaspoon
Oil
Pita bread

Soak garbanzos overnight or quick-soak; drain. Put ½ the garbanzos in a
food processor or blender with ½ the garlic, onion, cumin, coriander,
and parsley. Add salt, pepper, and ½ the cayenne; blend to a fine puree
and pour into a large mixing bowl. Repeat the same procedure with remaining garbanzos. Add baking powder to bowl and mix well. Shape
mixture into balls about the size of walnuts; flatten slightly. Deep fry in
oil until nicely browned, turning once. Serve in pita bread. Makes about
36 balls.

Egyptian Falafel

Garbanzos 1 cup
Green onions 3, chopped
Parsley ½ cup chopped (packed)
Garlic cloves 3, minced
Egg 1, beaten
Salt and pepper to taste
Baking soda ½ teaspoon
Ground cumin ½ teaspoon
Sesame seeds
Oil

Soak garbanzos overnight or quick-soak; drain. In a food grinder or food
processor, finely grind garbanzos with onions, parsley, and garlic. Add

egg and mix well. Season with salt and pepper, then add soda and cumin. Let stand at least 15 minutes. Shape mixture into tiny balls or 2-inch patties; pat a pinch of sesame seeds into each ball. Heat 1 inch of oil to about 370°; place balls in hot oil and fry until brown on all sides. Use as a filling in pita bread with shredded lettuce, chopped tomatoes, and other desired condiments; garnish with tahini sauce (a sesame seed sauce that can be purchased in specialty sections of supermarkets or in Middle Eastern grocery shops). Makes about 24 balls.

Note: Falafel balls can be made ahead and reheated in the oven.

Middle Eastern Falafel

Garbanzos 2 cups cooked or
  Canned garbanzos 16-ounce can, drained
Large onion 1, chopped
Garlic cloves 2, minced
Parsley 1 cup chopped
Green chili peppers 1 or 2, chopped (optional)
Yeast 1 package
Warm water ¼ cup
Salt 2 teaspoons or to taste
Pepper ½ teaspoon
Oil

Combine first 5 ingredients and blend or grind a little at a time. Dissolve yeast in warm water; add to garbanzo mixture with salt and pepper and mix thoroughly. Cover and let stand in a warm place for 1 to 2 hours, then refrigerate for 2 hours. Form into patties about 1½ inches in diameter. Deep fry in hot oil until patties are golden brown and crisp. Serve hot or at room temperature, in pita bread or as finger food. Makes 36 patties.

Garbanzos with Pimientos

Garbanzos   8 ounces
Beef stock   1 quart
Vienna sausages   5-ounce can
Water or beef stock
Salt and pepper   to taste
Whole pimientos   3, cut into thin strips
Oil
Bread crumbs   1 cup

Soak garbanzos in beef stock overnight, then simmer for 2 hours. Drop in whole sausages and cook until garbanzos are done, adding just enough water or stock to keep the beans from sticking (pot should be almost dry when beans are done). Add salt and pepper. Sauté pimientos in oil; add bread crumbs and sauté until crumbs are golden. Drain garbanzos if necessary and sprinkle crumb mixture over top. Serves 4.

Garbanzo Pot Pie

Medium onion   1, chopped
Celery   1 stalk, chopped
Green pepper   1 tablespoon chopped
Potato   1, peeled and cut into ½-inch cubes
Water
Garbanzos   1½ cups cooked
Cream of mushroom soup   10¾-ounce can
Frozen peas   1 cup
Salt   to taste
Chicken bouillon cube   1
Biscuit dough

Cook fresh vegetables with just enough water to make them tender; drain. Add next 5 ingredients and heat until bouillon dissolves. Put in a shallow baking dish and cover with biscuit dough cut into rounds. Bake at 400° about 10 to 12 minutes until biscuits are golden brown. Serves 6.

Lamb with Garbanzos

Ground lamb 1 pound
Oil 2 tablespoons
Onion 1 cup finely chopped
Garbanzos 2 cups cooked, liquid reserved, or
    Canned garbanzos 16-ounce can, liquid drained and reserved
Rice ¾ cup cooked
Curry powder 1 teaspoon
Water 1½ cups
Salt and pepper to taste

In a Dutch oven, brown lamb in oil with onion. Add remaining ingredients, including garbanzo liquid; cover tightly and simmer 30 minutes. Serves 4.

Pork Chop–Garbanzo Casserole

Large onion 1, chopped
Oil 2 tablespoons
Pork chops 4 to 6
Garbanzos 2 cups cooked, liquid reserved, or
    Canned garbanzos two 15-ounce cans
Cabbage 1 medium head, shredded
Salt and pepper to taste
Vinegar to taste

Cook onion in oil until golden. In a large skillet brown pork chops on both sides until almost done. Add onion, garbanzos (with liquid), and cabbage. Cover and cook over medium heat about 15 minutes until cabbage is tender. Add salt, pepper, and vinegar. Arrange on a serving platter and serve with apple cider. Serves 4 to 6.

Mexican Garbanzos

Garbanzos 8 ounces
Water
Bacon strips 3
Shortening 1 tablespoon
Onion 2 tablespoons chopped
Garlic clove 1, minced
Tomato sauce 1 cup
Cumin seeds 4
Chili powder to taste
Hot sausages 2, thinly sliced
Salt to taste
Parsley 2 tablespoons chopped

Soak garbanzos overnight or quick-soak; drain. Cook garbanzos in a generous amount of water. Remove the skins (they will slip off easily) and return the beans to their cooking water. Fry bacon until crisp; remove from pan and crumble. Add shortening to bacon fat. Add next 5 ingredients and cook for a few minutes to blend. Add to garbanzos and water. Add sausages, bacon, and salt; continue cooking until thick. Sprinkle with parsley and serve hot. Serves 6.

Garbanzo Casserole

Ground beef 1½ pounds
Salt 1 teaspoon
Pepper ½ teaspoon
Garlic salt ½ teaspoon
Large onions 2, chopped
Tomatoes 28-ounce can
Garbanzos 4 cups cooked or
    Canned garbanzos two 16-ounce cans, drained
Water chestnuts two 8-ounce cans, drained and sliced
Cheddar cheese ½ cup shredded

Brown meat. Add next 5 ingredients and simmer 30 minutes. Add garbanzos and water chestnuts, stir to blend, and pour into a 2½-quart casserole. Sprinkle cheese on top and bake uncovered at 350° for 30 minutes. Serves 6 to 8.

Totonac Stew

Garbanzos ½ cup
White beans ½ cup
Veal 1 pound, cut up
Lamb 1 pound, cut up
Pork loin 1 pound, cut up
Chicken 1, cut up
Ham 2 large slices, cut up
Chorizos 2, sliced
Garlic cloves 6, minced
Water
Large firm bananas 2, unpeeled, sliced
Green beans 1 cup
Cabbage ½ medium head, shredded
Small summer squash 3, sliced
Chayotes or potatoes 3, cut into large pieces
Onions 3, sliced
Ground cumin ¼ teaspoon
Saffron ¼ teaspoon
Salt and pepper to taste

Soak garbanzos overnight or quick-soak; drain. Put in a large kettle with next 7 ingredients and cover with water. Cook slowly for 3 hours. Add remaining ingredients, mixing saffron with a little water before adding to broth; cook until vegetables are tender. Serve in large soup bowls with hot fresh bread for dipping. Serves 12.

Madrid Feast

Garbanzos   8 ounces
Navy beans   8 ounces
Tender boiling chicken   1, whole
Beef heart   1 pound
Lean unsliced bacon   4 ounces
Uncooked ham   4 ounces
Salt and pepper   to taste
Water   5 to 6 quarts
Large onion   1, chopped
Chorizo   1 (optional)
Cabbage   1 small head
Medium potatoes   2 pounds
Chopped parsley or coriander leaves   garnish
Guacamole
Red salsa

Soak garbanzos overnight or quick-soak; drain. Put garbanzos in a muslin bag; put in a large pot with next 6 ingredients and cover with water. Bring to a boil, then simmer over low heat for 5 hours. Add chorizo, if desired. Remove 6 leaves from cabbage and chop; cut 4 potatoes into ½-inch cubes. Add chopped and whole cabbage and potatoes to bean mixture and cook about 40 minutes more. Remove chicken with a slotted server, cut into pieces, and place on a platter. Remove other meats, slice, arrange on the platter, and garnish with chopped parsley. Put beans, broth, and vegetables in a heated tureen and sprinkle with fresh parsley or fresh coriander leaves. Serve with bowls of guacamole and red salsa. Serves 8 to 10.

Spanish Cocido

Fresh beef brisket 2½ pounds
Carrots 4, peeled
Leeks 4, sliced
Salt pork 2 pounds, cut into cubes
Chorizo 2 pounds
Garbanzos 7 cups cooked
Rosemary 1 teaspoon
Freshly ground pepper ½ teaspoon
Water
Cabbage 1 large head, cut into 8 wedges
Potatoes 6 to 8 servings, boiled

Place first 8 ingredients in a large pot and cover with water. Bring to a boil; reduce heat, cover, and simmer about 3 hours. Add cabbage and continue simmering until cabbage is just tender. Adjust seasonings to taste. Remove and slice beef and sausage; remove vegetables and arrange on a platter with sliced meat and salt pork. Surround with boiled potatoes. Serve garbanzos with broth in soup bowls. A coarse salt, a variety of mustards, and hot breads traditionally are served with this meal. Serves 6 to 8.

Vegetable Curry

Oil   ¼ cup
Cumin seeds   1½ teaspoons
Onions   2 cups chopped
Chopped green chili peppers   4-ounce can
Salt   1 tablespoon
Ground coriander   2 tablespoons
Turmeric   1 teaspoon
Bay leaf   1
Medium potatoes   2, chopped (about 1½ cups)
Water   ¼ cup
Medium carrots   2, thinly sliced
Cauliflower   2 cups flowerettes
Frozen peas   10-ounce package
Medium zucchini   1, thinly sliced
Garbanzos   2 to 3 cups cooked, liquid reserved, or
    Canned garbanzos   20-ounce can, undrained
Yogurt Sauce

Heat oil in a large skillet over medium heat and brown cumin seeds for almost 1 minute. Reduce heat and add next 6 ingredients; cook 2 minutes. Add potatoes and water; cover and simmer over low heat 10 minutes. Add carrots and cauliflower; cover and simmer 5 to 7 minutes more. Add peas, zucchini, and garbanzos (with liquid); cover and simmer another 10 minutes. Remove bay leaf. Serve with Yogurt Sauce. Serves 6.

Yogurt Sauce

Plain yogurt   2 cups
Large cucumber   1, peeled, seeded, and grated
Salt   ¼ teaspoon
Ground cumin   ⅛ teaspoon

Combine all ingredients in a bowl and refrigerate until serving time. Makes 2½ cups.

All-American Baked Beans

Great Northern or navy beans 3 cups
Water
Boiling water
Lean salt pork 4 ounces
Small onion 1, thinly sliced
Salt 1 tablespoon
Sugar 3 tablespoons
Dry mustard ½ teaspoon
Molasses ⅓ cup

Cover beans with water and soak overnight or quick-soak. Bring to a boil, then reduce heat and simmer until beans are very tender. Drain, reserving liquid. Meanwhile, pour boiling water over salt pork and let stand 10 minutes; drain. Remove rind and discard; cut remainder into small cubes and place in a large bean pot with onion. Dissolve salt, sugar, mustard, and molasses in a cup of the hot bean liquid and put in bean pot. Add beans with just enough of their liquid to cover; stir gently. Cover and bake at 250° for 6 to 8 hours. Add hot bean liquid or boiling water as needed to cover beans. Serves 8 to 10.

Booze Baked Beans

Thickly sliced bacon 8 ounces, cut into 2-inch pieces
All-American Baked Beans 8 cups or
    Canned baked beans four 16-ounce cans
Dry mustard 2 teaspoons
Ginger ¼ teaspoon
Rum or bourbon ½ cup
Strong coffee ¼ cup
Dark brown sugar* ½ cup
Sliced pineapple 8-ounce can, drained

Fry bacon until crisp. Remove bacon from pan and drain on paper towels. Combine beans, mustard, and ginger in a 3-quart casserole; cover and bake at 350° for 45 minutes. Stir in rum, coffee, and brown sugar. Cut pineapple slices in half and arrange with bacon on top of beans. Return to oven and bake uncovered until pineapple is golden brown. Serves 8.
* Reduce or eliminate brown sugar if beans are already quite sweet.

Baked Beans with Beef

Great Northern beans   8 ounces
Water   3 cups
Ham hock   1
Medium onions   2, sliced
Butter or oil   1 tablespoon
Ground chuck   1 pound
Italian-style pear-shaped tomatoes   14-ounce can
Brown sugar   2 tablespoons
Dry mustard   1 teaspoon
Mustard seed   1 teaspoon
Chili powder   1 teaspoon
Worcestershire sauce   1 teaspoon
Salt and pepper   to taste

Combine beans and water and soak overnight or quick-soak, then cook 1 hour. Add ham hock and continue to cook until beans are tender, adding more water as needed. Sauté onions in butter until golden; remove onions from pan and cook beef in same pan until crumbly. Add next 6 ingredients and simmer 10 minutes. Combine with beans in a 2½-quart casserole. Add salt and pepper and onions. Bake at 400° for 30 minutes, or until thickened. Serves 6 to 8.

Italian Baked Beans

Great Northern beans   1 cup
Boiling water   3 cups
Garlic clove   1, minced
Salt   2 teaspoons
Pepper   to taste
Small bay leaf   1
Tomatoes   8-ounce can, undrained and chopped
Onions   2, chopped
Green pepper   1, seeded and chopped
Parsley   3 tablespoons chopped
Dried basil   1 teaspoon
Extra-sharp Romano cheese   2 tablespoons grated
Italian-seasoned bread crumbs   1 tablespoon

Soak beans overnight or quick-soak; drain. Combine first 6 ingredients and bring to a boil. Lower heat, cover, and simmer about 1 hour until beans are tender, stirring occasionally. Drain beans; remove bay leaf. Put beans in a baking dish and mix in next 5 ingredients. Cover and bake at 350° for 1 hour. Sprinkle top with cheese and bread crumbs and bake uncovered 30 minutes more. Serves 4.

Mixed Bean Casserole with Ham

Ham 1 to 2 cups cooked and chopped
Onion 1 cup chopped
Garlic cloves 2, minced
Oil 2 tablespoons
Kidney beans 2 cups cooked or
    Canned kidney beans 15-ounce can, drained
Small white beans 2 cups cooked or
    Canned cannellini beans 16-ounce can, drained
Garbanzos 3 cups cooked or
    Canned garbanzos 20-ounce can, drained
Catsup ½ cup
Prepared mustard 2 tablespoons
Maple syrup 2 tablespoons (optional)
Dry white wine ¼ cup
Dark brown sugar 2 tablespoons
Salt 1 teaspoon
Pepper dash
Ground cloves dash

Sauté ham, onion, and garlic in oil until onion is soft; add beans. Combine remaining ingredients in a bowl. Pour over ham and bean mixture; toss gently. Pour into a 2-quart casserole and bake at 350° for 45 minutes. Serves 6.

Kidney Bean Casserole

Large garlic clove   1, minced
Large onion   1, chopped
Bacon drippings or oil   ¼ cup
Kidney beans   4 cups cooked or
     Canned kidney beans   two 16-ounce cans, drained
Tomato paste   1 tablespoon
Red wine   1½ cups
Ham   1½ cups cooked and cut into cubes
Salt and pepper   to taste

Sauté garlic and onion in bacon drippings until just tender. Add beans, tomato paste, and wine. Bring to a boil, then reduce heat and simmer 10 minutes. Add ham and heat thoroughly. Add salt and pepper, and more wine if moisture is needed. Serves 6 to 8.

Kidney Bean and Pork Sausage Casserole

Kidney beans   6 cups cooked, liquid reserved, or
     Canned kidney beans   three 16-ounce cans
Butter   ¼ cup
Medium onions   2, chopped
Sliced pimientos   two 4-ounce jars
Brown sugar   ½ cup
Salt   2 teaspoons
Pepper   1 teaspoon
Bulk sausage   8 ounces

Place beans and liquid in a 2½-quart casserole and set aside. In a large frying pan, melt butter and cook onions and pimientos over low heat for 15 minutes. Stir onion mixture into beans. Add brown sugar, salt and pepper and stir until blended. Brown sausage and drain off fat. Top casserole with sausage, cover, and bake at 350° for 1 hour. Uncover and bake about 10 minutes until sausage is crisp. Serves 6 to 8.

Kidney Bean Patties

Kidney beans 1 cup
Water 1 quart
Oil 2 tablespoons
Chives ½ cup chopped
Parsley 2 tablespoons chopped
Lemon 1, thinly sliced

Combine beans and water; soak overnight or quick-soak. Cook over low heat until very tender; drain liquid and reserve. Heat oil in a skillet and add chives, parsley, and drained beans. Cook, mashing beans with a fork. When beans are well mashed, add bean liquid and cook over low heat until liquid has almost evaporated. Form into patties, and top each with a lemon slice before serving. Serves 4.

Refried Beans with Rice

Onion ¾ cup chopped
Garlic clove 1, minced
Olive oil 3 tablespoons
Red kidney beans 5 cups cooked
Tomato paste 2 tablespoons
Salt ½ teaspoon
Sugar ½ teaspoon
Freshly ground pepper ¼ teaspoon
Parsley 1 tablespoon chopped
Rice 3 cups cooked

Sauté onion and garlic in oil for 3 minutes. Add next 5 ingredients; cook and stir over low heat for 15 minutes. Sprinkle with parsley and serve over hot rice. Serves 6.

Haitian Bean Dish

Kidney beans 1 cup
Water 3 cups
Salt 1½ teaspoons
Onion 1, chopped
Garlic clove 1, minced
Parsley 3 sprigs, chopped
Oil or bacon drippings 1 tablespoon
Pepper ½ teaspoon
Ground cloves ¼ teaspoon
Oil or bacon drippings 1 tablespoon
Water or broth
Rice 1 cup

Cover beans with water and boil for 5 minutes. Add salt and let stand for 1 hour. Drain, reserving liquid. Sauté onion, garlic, and parsley in oil. Add pepper and cloves and pour into a casserole. Heat remaining tablespoon of oil in skillet and sauté beans for 5 minutes over medium heat; add to casserole. Add enough water or broth to bean liquid to make 5½ cups. Pour over beans. Cover and bake at 250° for 2 hours, or until beans become soft. Stir in rice and bake 1 hour more, adding water or broth as needed. Serves 6 to 8.

New Version of Old Spanish Bean Pot

Bacon strips 3, chopped
Yellow onion 1, sliced
Red kidney beans 8 to 9 cups cooked, liquid drained and reserved
Syrup from canned peaches ½ cup
Cider vinegar 2 tablespoons
Strong coffee ¼ cup
Garlic clove 1, minced
Rosemary pinch
Bay leaf 1, crumbled
Ground cloves ¼ teaspoon
Thyme pinch
Salt 1 teaspoon
Dry mustard 2 teaspoons
Cayenne ¼ teaspoon
Pumpkin 1 cup cut into 1½-inch cubes
Bacon strips 4
Brandy jigger

Fry bacon until crisp, then fry onion in bacon drippings until golden. Combine bacon and onion with beans; add syrup, vinegar, and coffee. Blend next 8 ingredients and stir into beans. Pour bean mixture into a very large, greased casserole and fold in pumpkin. Bake in a very slow oven (250° to 300°) for 1 hour. Put 4 strips of bacon on top, add bean liquid if needed, and bake 30 minutes more. Just before serving add brandy, stirring it in the casserole from the bottom up. Serve with a side dish of peaches in place of a salad. Serves 12 to 14.

Enchiladas with Bean Sauce

Kidney beans 2 cups cooked or
   Canned kidney beans 15-ounce can, drained
Water or stock
Butter 2 tablespoons, melted
Onion 2 tablespoons chopped
Chili sauce to taste
Salt to taste
Tortillas
Chicken or sausage 1 cup cooked and chopped
Cheddar cheese 1 cup grated

Mash beans with enough water or stock to keep them moist. Add next 4 ingredients and cook until mixture is creamy. Butter a large baking dish. Spread a large tortilla with a spoonful of bean mixture and a layer of meat; sprinkle with grated cheese. Fold and put in baking dish 1 layer at a time. Sprinkle cheese on top layer and bake at 300° for 10 to 15 minutes. Serves 8.

Tortillas

White cornmeal ½ cup
Salt ½ teaspoon
Milk ½ cup
Oil 2 tablespoons
Eggs 3

Mix all ingredients. Grease a 7-inch frying pan and drop 1 tablespoon of tortilla mixture onto pan. Tilt pan to form a thin round pancake. When bottom is done, turn and cook other side. Keep soft and warm by placing cooked tortillas on a plate over a bowl of hot water.

Pineapple Beans with Meatballs

Ground beef 1½ pounds
Medium onion 1, chopped
Salt 1 teaspoon
Oil 2 tablespoons
Catsup 1 cup
Water ½ cup
Brown sugar ¼ cup
Vinegar 2 tablespoons
Dry mustard 2 teaspoons
Kidney beans 2 cups cooked, liquid reserved, or
    Canned kidney beans 16-ounce can
Pork and beans 4 cups or
    Canned pork and beans two 16-ounce cans
Pineapple chunks 15¼-ounce can, drained

Mix meat, onion, and salt; form into small balls and brown in oil. Remove meatballs from pan. Add next 5 ingredients to oil in pan and stir to blend; cook 5 minutes. Combine beans (with liquid) and pineapple in a 2½-quart casserole, reserving ½ cup pineapple. Place meatballs and reserved pineapple on top of beans. Pour catsup mixture over all. Bake at 375° for 45 minutes. Serves 8 to 10.

Mexican-Style Beef

Brown rice 1 cup
Beef bouillon cube 1
Medium onion 1, thinly sliced
Butter or margarine ½ cup
Ground beef 1 pound
Garlic clove 1, minced
Dry mustard 2 teaspoons
Chili powder 1 tablespoon
Salt 1 teaspoon
Tomatoes 16-ounce can
Kidney beans 2 cups cooked, liquid reserved, or
   Canned kidney beans 16-ounce can
Paprika 1 teaspoon
Parmesan cheese ¼ cup grated

Cook rice according to package directions, adding bouillon cube to cooking water. Sauté onion in butter. Crumble beef and add to onion with garlic, mustard, chili powder, and salt. Cook until meat loses pinkness. Layer ½ the meat mixture in the bottom of a 2-quart casserole. Spread cooked rice over meat. Spoon tomatoes over rice; spoon beans (with liquid) over tomatoes. Put remaining meat on top. Combine paprika and cheese and sprinkle over casserole. Bake uncovered at 350° for 30 minutes. Serves 8.

Quick London Chili-Bean Tacos

Ground beef 1 pound
Green pepper ½ cup chopped
Onion ¼ cup chopped
Chili powder 1 tablespoon
Mayonnaise ½ cup
Kidney or pinto beans 2 cups cooked
Shredded lettuce
English muffins 6, split, toasted, and buttered
Shredded Cheddar cheese topping

Brown meat; remove from pan. Cook green pepper and onion in the fat left in the pan. Drain off fat. Stir in chili powder and mayonnaise. Heat through and add meat and beans, mixing well. Place lettuce on toasted muffins and spoon on beef-bean mixture. Sprinkle with cheese. Serves 6.

Hamburger with Chili and Beans

Red kidney beans 1 pound
Water
Onion 1
Salt to taste
Shortening 1 tablespoon
Onion 2 tablespoons chopped
Shortening 3 tablespoons
Chili powder 1 tablespoon or
　　Canned molé powder 3 tablespoons
Ground beef 2 pounds
Fresh or canned tomatoes 4, chopped
Cornstarch 2 tablespoons
Water
Small bay leaf 1
Dry oregano pinch
Tortillas

Soak beans overnight or quick-soak; drain. Cook beans in water with whole onion, salt, and 1 tablespoon shortening until beans are soft. Sauté chopped onion in 3 tablespoons shortening until soft; add chili powder and meat and cook until meat is no longer pink. Add tomatoes and heat through, then add cornstarch mixed with a little water. Add bay leaf and oregano and cook until thickened; remove bay leaf. Serve with hot tortillas. Serves 6 to 8.

Simple Chili

Ground beef 2 pounds
Bulk sausage 1 pound
Medium onions 2, chopped
Garlic cloves 3, minced
Tomatoes two 16-ounce cans
Tomato sauce 1½ cups
Kidney beans 8 cups cooked, liquid reserved
Chili powder to taste
Ground cumin to taste
Oregano to taste
Cayenne to taste

Brown meats; add remaining ingredients and simmer over low heat about 3 hours, occasionally skimming fat from surface. Serves 8 to 10.

Chili Beans with Macaroni

Kidney beans 1½ cups
Water 6 cups
Oil ¼ cup
Celery with leaves ½ cup thinly sliced
Onion ½ cup chopped
Garlic cloves 3, minced
Tomatoes 16-ounce can
Salt 3 teaspoons
Chili powder 2 teaspoons
Pepper ¼ teaspoon
Small elbow macaroni 1 cup
Sharp Cheddar cheese 1 cup shredded
Onion ½ cup chopped

Soak beans in water overnight or quick-soak, then simmer over moderate heat for 1 hour. Add oil, celery, onion, and garlic. Cover and cook until beans are tender. Stir in next 5 ingredients; cook, stirring occasionally, about 10 minutes until macaroni is tender, adding more water if needed. Sprinkle with cheese and onion and serve. Serves 6.

Medley Acapulco

Oil 2 tablespoons
Medium onion 1, finely chopped
Green pepper 1, seeded and chopped
Pimiento 4-ounce jar, drained and chopped
Green chili peppers 4-ounce can, seeded and chopped
Tomatoes 16-ounce can, drained and chopped
Kidney beans 2 cups cooked, liquid drained and ¼ cup reserved
Corn 16-ounce can, liquid drained and ¼ cup reserved
Tabasco sauce ¼ teaspoon (optional)
Pepper ½ teaspoon
Paprika 1 teaspoon
Chili powder ½ teaspoon
Salt to taste

Heat oil in a 3-quart saucepan. Add onion and green pepper and sauté, stirring constantly, until soft. Add remaining ingredients and simmer 15 minutes, stirring occasionally. Serves 4.

Kidney Bean Chili

Kidney beans   4 cups cooked or
   Canned kidney beans   two 16-ounce cans, drained
Chili powder   2 tablespoons
Red wine, beer, or vermouth   ½ cup
Meat or fowl   1 to 2 cups chopped
Chopped green onions   garnish (optional)
Shredded cheese   garnish (optional)

Combine first 4 ingredients and heat thoroughly. Garnish with green onions and cheese and serve. Serves 6 to 8.

Armenian Lentil Patties

Lentils   1⅓ cups
Onion   1 cup chopped
Large garlic cloves   2, crushed
Water   1 quart
Bulgur   1 cup
Parsley   ¼ cup chopped
Oil   2 tablespoons
Salt   1¾ teaspoons
Paprika   1 teaspoon
Pepper   ¼ teaspoon
Parsley   1 cup chopped
Green onions with tops   1 cup finely chopped

In a covered pot, cook lentils, onion, and garlic in water about 25 minutes until lentils are tender. Add next 5 ingredients and mix well; cover and simmer over low heat 2 minutes. Cool to lukewarm. Add pepper and stir well. Divide mixture into 18 portions and shape into patties. Mix parsley and green onions and roll patties in mixture. Serves 6.

Health Burgers

Lentils ½ cup
Water 1½ cups
Salt 1¼ teaspoons
Butter 1 tablespoon
Green onions 1 cup chopped
Garlic clove 1, crushed
Fresh bread crumbs ¾ cup
Wheat germ ¼ cup
Walnuts 1 cup finely chopped
Eggs 2
Steak sauce 4 teaspoons
Salt ½ teaspoon
Tabasco sauce 3 drops
Butter 2 tablespoons
Sliced tomatoes (optional)
Sliced onions (optional)

Over medium heat, cook lentils with water and salt about 25 minutes, or until lentils are tender. Drain and mash lentils. In a medium skillet, melt 1 tablespoon butter. Add onions and garlic and sauté about 3 minutes. Stir in lentils and next 7 ingredients. Shape into patties and fry in 2 tablespoons butter until patties are brown, lifting patties occasionally to prevent sticking. Serve with sliced tomatoes and onions. Serves 4.

Lentil–Nut Loaf

Small onion 1, finely chopped
Oil 3 tablespoons
Wheat germ ½ cup
Lentils 2 cups cooked
Walnuts ½ cup chopped
Whole wheat bread crumbs ½ cup
Eggs 2, beaten
Water ½ cup
Vinegar 1 tablespoon
Sesame seeds

Sauté onion in oil until soft; add remaining ingredients except sesame seeds. Press into a greased loaf pan and sprinkle with sesame seeds. Cover and bake at 350° for 30 minutes; uncover and bake 10 minutes more. Serves 6 to 8.

Campfire Cauldron

Chicken or turkey franks   6 to 8, each cut into 4 pieces
Rice   ½ cup
Large onion   1, sliced
Garlic cloves   2, minced
Carrots   2, thinly sliced
Celery   2 stalks, cut into 1-inch pieces
Oil   2 tablespoons
Lentils   8 ounces
Water   3 quarts
Beef bouillon cubes   6
Tomato paste   6-ounce can
Salt   1 teaspoon
Pepper   ½ teaspoon
Bay leaf   1
Dried thyme   ¼ teaspoon

Sauté first 6 ingredients in oil until rice is golden. Add remaining ingredients and cover. Bring to a boil, then simmer until lentils are tender. Remove bay leaf and serve. Serves 8.

One-Pot Beef and Lentil Supper

Lean ground beef   1½ pounds
Large onion   1, chopped
Dry salami   4 ounces, chopped
Lentils   1 pound
Italian seasoning or oregano leaves   1 teaspoon
Pumpkin pie spice   ½ teaspoon
Beef bouillon cubes   4
Water   6 cups
Salt   to taste
Chopped parsley   garnish

Crumble beef into a 5- to 6-quart Dutch oven and cook over medium heat until browned. Add onion and cook until onion is limp. Spoon off fat and discard. Add next 7 ingredients and simmer until lentils are tender. Garnish with chopped parsley. Serves 6 to 8.

Herbed Lentils and Rice

Chicken broth 2⅔ cups
Lentils ¾ cup
Onion ¾ cup chopped
Brown rice ½ cup
Dry white wine ¼ cup
Dried basil ½ teaspoon
Salt ¼ teaspoon
Dried oregano ¼ teaspoon
Dried thyme ¼ teaspoon
Garlic powder ⅛ teaspoon
Pepper ½ teaspoon
Swiss cheese 2 ounces, shredded
Swiss cheese 2 ounces, cut into 8 strips

Combine all ingredients except cheese strips and turn into an ungreased 1½-quart casserole. Cover and bake at 350° about 1½ hours until lentils and rice are cooked, stirring twice. Place cheese strips on top of the lentil-rice mixture. Bake uncovered 2 to 3 minutes until cheese melts. Serves 4.

Honey-Baked Lentils

Lentils 1 pound, cooked, liquid drained and 1 cup reserved
Dry mustard 1 teaspoon
Ginger ½ teaspoon
Soy sauce 1 tablespoon
Onion ½ cup chopped
Honey ½ cup

Combine all ingredients except honey and pour into a baking dish. Pour honey over lentil mixture; cover and bake at 350° for 1 hour. Uncover and continue baking about 15 to 20 minutes until top is nicely browned. Serves 6.

Wednesday Lentil Casserole

Lentils   2 cups
Water
Onion   1
Garlic cloves   2
Bay leaf   1
Ham   6 slices
Leftover chicken and stuffing   about 2 cups
Chicken broth   1 cup
Buttered crumbs   topping
Grated Parmesan cheese   topping

Soak lentils overnight or quick-soak; drain. Cover lentils with water. Slit onion in 2 places and insert garlic cloves into slits; add with bay leaf to lentils. Simmer gently until lentils are tender. Drain, reserving liquid; discard bay leaf and onion. In a casserole, layer ⅓ of the lentils, the ham, another ⅓ of the lentils, the chicken and stuffing, and top with the remaining ⅓ of the lentils. Mix the liquid from the lentils and the chicken broth and pour over all. Cover and bake at 350° for 30 minutes. Remove cover and sprinkle with crumbs and cheese; bake until topping is crisp. Serves 6 to 8.

Curried Lentils on Rice

Lentils   1 cup
Stock or bouillon   2 cups
Salt   ½ teaspoon
Onion   1, sliced
Curry powder   1 teaspoon
Rice   1½ cups cooked

Soak lentils overnight or quick-soak; drain. Cook slowly in stock with salt, onion, and curry powder for 1 hour, or until lentils are tender and mixture is like thick soup. Serve on hot rice. Serves 4.

Spanish Drunken Eggs

Lima beans 2 cups cooked
Bacon strips 6
Eggs 6
Salt and pepper to taste
Butter 3 tablespoons, melted
White wine ¼ cup

Press beans through a sieve or puree in a blender or food processor; press into a buttered shallow baking dish. Cook bacon until almost crisp; drain. Lay strips on top of beans. Break eggs over bacon; season with salt and pepper. Mix butter and wine and drizzle over the eggs. Bake at 325° for 12 minutes, or until eggs are set. Serves 6.

Limas with Chilis

Green chili peppers 4-ounce can or
   Fresh green chili peppers 4
Monterey Jack cheese 4 ounces
Flour 2 tablespoons
Onion 2 tablespoons chopped
Salt 1 teaspoon
Pepper ⅛ teaspoon
Oregano leaves ½ teaspoon
Basil leaves ½ teaspoon
Sour cream ½ cup
Small lima beans 4 cups cooked, liquid drained and 1 cup reserved
Butter or margarine 1 tablespoon

Scrape seeds and hot membranes from the peppers; cut cheese into 4 strips and place a strip inside each pepper. Combine next 7 ingredients in a medium bowl. Slowly stir in bean liquid until well mixed. Add beans, folding in to coat. Spoon bean mixture into a 1½-quart shallow baking dish; top with cheese-stuffed peppers. Bake at 350° for 30 minutes, or until bubbly. Serves 4.

Puchero

Lima beans 1 cup
Water
Butter 2 tablespoons
Cooked ham 1 pound, cut into 1-inch cubes
Pork shoulder 1½ pounds, cooked and cut into 1-inch cubes
Hot water 1½ cups
Lemon juice ¼ cup
Pepper ½ teaspoon
Bacon strips 6, chopped and cooked
Medium onions 4, chopped
Medium green pepper 1, seeded and chopped
Celery 4 cups chopped
Bay leaf 1
Cabbage 1 medium head, chopped

Combine beans and water to cover and soak overnight or quick-soak; do not drain. Melt butter in a large pan; brown ham and pork in butter for 10 minutes. Add hot water, lemon juice, and pepper and simmer 1 hour. Add next 5 ingredients and undrained beans. Simmmer 30 minutes more, or until vegetables are tender. Add cabbage and continue to simmer for 15 minutes, or until cabbage is tender. Remove bay leaf and discard. Serves 6 to 8.

Lima Beans and Dried Beef

Carrots 4, sliced
Large onion 1, sliced
Oil 1 tablespoon
Dried beef 4-ounce package
Flour 2 tablespoons
Salt 1 teaspoon
Lima beans 1 pound, cooked, liquid drained and reserved

Cook carrots and onion in oil until onion is golden. Tear dried beef into small pieces and add to vegetable mixture; cook 2 minutes more. Blend in flour and salt and stir until thick. Put beans in a casserole; pour meat and vegetable mixture over beans, adding just enough bean liquid to cover. Cover casserole and bake at 250° for 2 hours, adding more liquid as needed. Serves 4 to 6.

Beef Shank and Bean Trio

Lima or Great Northern beans 4 ounces
Red pinto beans 4 ounces
Water 3 cups
Beef shanks cross cuts 3 (about 2 pounds)
Medium onion 1, coarsely chopped
Salt 2 teaspoons
Sugar 2 teaspoons
Crushed red pepper ⅛ teaspoon
Tomatoes 16-ounce can
Flour 2 tablespoons
Green beans 16-ounce can, drained

Place beans in a Dutch oven and add water; soak overnight or quick-soak; do not drain. Place shanks in pot and push them deep to cover. Add onion, salt, sugar, and red pepper; cover and simmer 2½ hours. Drain tomatoes, reserving liquid. Stir liquid into flour to blend; gradually add flour mixture to beans and stir until thickened. Add tomatoes and green beans and continue cooking 15 minutes more. Serves 6.

Jewish Cholent

Lima or navy beans 1 cup
Water 2 quarts
Coarse barley* ½ cup
Shortribs, plate, or beef brisket 2 pounds
Ginger 1 teaspoon
Garlic powder ½ teaspoon
Salt 1 tablespoon
Pepper ¼ teaspoon

(Because no cooking may be done on the Sabbath, this dish is prepared on Thursday and Friday for serving on Saturday.) Soak beans in water overnight on Thursday, or for at least 6 hours on Friday. Add remaining ingredients and bring to a boil. Reduce heat and simmer 30 minutes. Remove meat and cut into serving-sized pieces; place in a large Dutch oven or casserole with bean mixture. Cover tightly and set in a very cool oven (temperature should not exceed 250°) until noon on Saturday. Serve in soup bowls. Serves 8.
* Six peeled and quartered potatoes may be substituted for barley if desired.

Vegetarian Cholent

Large onions 3, sliced
Garlic cloves 2, crushed
Oil 3 tablespoons
Lima beans 1 pound, cooked
Potatoes 4, peeled and quartered
Salt 1 tablespoon
Paprika 2 teaspoons
Pepper ½ teaspoon
Bay leaf 1
Boiling water

In a Dutch oven, sauté onions and garlic in oil until tender. Add next 6 ingredients; add boiling water to cover completely. Cover tightly and bake at 300° for 6 to 8 hours or overnight. Discard bay leaf and serve. Serves 6.

Barbecued Lima Beans

Lima beans 12 ounces
Water
Smoked ham or salt pork piece
Garlic clove 1
Large onion 1, chopped
Garlic clove 1, minced
Bacon drippings ½ cup
Prepared mustard 1½ tablespoons
Worcestershire sauce 2 tablespoons
Salt to taste
Tomato soup 10¾-ounce can
Vinegar ¼ cup
Chili powder 1 tablespoon
Bacon strips garnish

Soak beans overnight or quick-soak; drain. Cook beans in water with ham and garlic clove until tender. Drain, reserving 2 cups liquid. Sauté onion and minced garlic in bacon drippings. When onion is clear add next 6 ingredients and reserved liquid. In greased casserole, alternate layers of beans and sauce. Place bacon strips on top of casserole and bake 40 minutes at 300°. Turn off heat and leave casserole in oven until serving time. Serves 6.

Supper Party Lima Beans

Baby lima beans 1 pound
Water
Tomato juice 2 cups
Dark brown sugar ¾ cup
Salt 1 teaspoon
Pepper ¼ teaspoon
Very fatty boneless beef 8 ounces
Tomato juice ½ cup

Soak beans overnight or quick-soak; drain. Cook beans in water until tender but firm; drain. In a small saucepan, heat tomato juice, brown sugar, salt, and pepper until sugar dissolves. Cut meat into very thin strips, having some fat and some lean on each strip. In a casserole or bean pot, alternate layers of beans, meat, and hot tomato mixture. Cover pot tightly and bake at 325° for 2 hours. Remove cover, cool, then refrigerate at least 24 hours (or the beans may be frozen at this point). One hour before serving remove from refrigerator (or remove from freezer 2 hours before serving); lightly stir in remaining tomato juice. Cover tightly and reheat at 325° for 1 hour. Serves 8.

Parve (Jewish Baked Beans)

Navy beans 1 pound, cooked
Tomato sauce 1 cup
Vegetable shortening or kosher margarine ¼ cup, melted
Molasses 1 tablespoon
Salt and pepper to taste

Combine all ingredients. Place in a 1½-quart casserole, cover tightly, and bake at 350° for 1 hour. Serves 7 to 9.

Portuguese Beans

Pink beans 1 pound
Water 5 cups
Bacon strips 5, chopped
Large onion 1, chopped
Garlic clove 1, minced
Cinnamon ½ teaspoon
Ground cloves ¼ teaspoon
Ground allspice ¼ teaspoon
Cumin seeds 1 teaspoon, crushed
Molasses 2 tablespoons
Salt 1 tablespoon
Pepper ¼ teaspoon
Italian tomatoes 28-ounce can

In a 5-quart kettle, cover beans with water and soak overnight or quick-soak; do not drain. Fry bacon until brown. Add onion and garlic and cook over low heat until onion is limp and golden. Stir bacon mixture and remaining ingredients into beans, breaking the tomatoes into small pieces. Bring to a boil, then cover and simmer 1½ hours. Uncover and simmer about 45 minutes more until beans are tender and sauce is thick. Serves 8 to 10.

Rancho Verde Chili Beans

Small pink beans 3 pounds
Meat stock or bouillon 6 quarts
Medium ham bone 1
Water
Sliced bacon 1 pound, chopped
Garlic cloves 8, minced
Onion ¾ cup finely chopped
Lean ground chuck 3 pounds
Link sausages 1-pound package
Mushrooms 3 cups chopped
Solid-pack tomatoes 6 cups, broken
Tomato paste two 6-ounce cans
Spanish tomato sauce two 8-ounce cans
Oregano 1½ teaspoons
Salt 2 tablespoons or to taste
Ground cumin 2 teaspoons
Chili con carne seasoning 2 tablespoons
Flour 3 tablespoons

Soak beans overnight or quick-soak; drain. Combine beans, stock, and ham bone; add water, if necessary, to cover. Cover and cook 2 hours. Remove bone. Fry bacon until crisp and add to beans. Sauté garlic and onion in bacon drippings and add with drippings to beans. Form ground chuck into a large patty and broil; broil sausages. Cut patty and sausages into bite-sized pieces and add to beans. Stir in remaining ingredients except flour. Cook about 3 to 4 hours until beans are tender. Adjust seasonings to taste. Mix flour with a small amount of bean liquid to make a paste; add paste to beans and cook about 30 minutes more. Serves 20 or more.

Bean Enchiladas

Pinto beans   ⅔ cup
Water
Onion   ½ cup chopped
Chopped green chili peppers   half 4-ounce can
Garlic salt   1 teaspoon
Salt   ½ teaspoon
Red enchilada sauce   one and one-half 10-ounce cans
Corn tortillas   10 to 12
Oil
Cheddar cheese   1 cup shredded
Green onions   ¼ cup chopped
Sour cream   topping (optional)

Combine beans and water and soak overnight or quick-soak. Cook in soaking water 1 to 2 hours, or until tender; drain. Mash beans in a large bowl. Add onion, peppers, garlic salt, salt, and 2 tablespoons enchilada sauce; mix well. Spread ¼ cup enchilada sauce over the bottom of an 8 by 12-inch baking dish. One at a time, soften each tortilla in hot oil and drain on paper towels. Place a spoonful of bean mixture on tortilla and roll up; place seam side down in the baking dish. Pour remaining sauce evenly over tortillas and sprinkle with cheese. Bake at 350° for 20 minutes, or until cheese is bubbly. Sprinkle with green onions before serving. Pass sour cream as an additional topping if desired. Serves 5 or 6.

Haricot of Lamb

Pinto beans or white navy beans   1 pound
Water
Whole cloves   2
Onion   1
Salt   1 teaspoon
Pepper   dash
Bay leaf   1
Garlic clove   1
Lamb shoulder   2½ pounds, cut into 1½-inch cubes
Flour
Olive oil   2 to 6 tablespoons
Garlic cloves   2, finely minced
Leeks   3, sliced
Ground thyme   1 teaspoon
Broth or red wine
Buttered crumbs

Soak beans overnight or quick-soak; drain. Put beans in a large pot; cover with water. Insert cloves halfway into onion and add to beans with next 4 ingredients. Bring to a boil; simmer until beans are tender. Drain; discard onion and bay leaf. Dust lamb with flour. Brown in oil, then add garlic, leeks, thyme, and broth to cover. Bring to a boil, then reduce heat and simmer, covered, about 1 to 2 hours until lamb is tender. Combine lamb mixture with beans. Place in casserole and bake uncovered for 45 to 60 minutes, basting with additional broth. Sprinkle with buttered crumbs and bake 15 minutes more. Serves 5 to 6.

Smoky Barbecued Pinto Beans

Pinto beans   2 pounds
Water   about 2 quarts
Unsliced bacon without rind   1 pound, cut into ¾-inch cubes
Medium onions   3, sliced
Italian tomatoes   28-ounce can
Salt   2 teaspoons
Pepper   ½ teaspoon
Chili powder   2 tablespoons
Oregano leaves   1 teaspoon
Dry mustard   2 tablespoons
Cumin seed   ⅛ teaspoon
Water   3 tablespoons
Dark molasses   1 cup

Combine beans and water and soak overnight or quick-soak. Add enough water to cover, and bring to a boil. Add bacon, onions, and tomatoes and return to a boil, then reduce heat and simmer about 2 hours until beans are tender. Mix next 6 ingredients and make a paste by slowly adding the water. Mix molasses into paste. Put beans in a 6- to 8-quart container; stir in paste. If using a smoker, follow directions for smoking food uncovered at 300° for 2 hours. If using a barbecue, arrange glowing coals 6 inches below the baking container and 1½ inches outside its circumference; sprinkle coals with hickory chips. Cook beans uncovered in the center of the grill. Cover the barbecue and adjust to maintain *very low* cooking heat for 2 hours, adding more chips or charcoal as needed. Stir beans every ½ hour to keep them from sticking. If using an oven, place beans in the center of the oven and bake at 300° for 2 hours. Season to taste with salt, pepper, and smoke flavoring. Makes 4 quarts.

Traditional Chili

Pinto beans   2 cups
Water
Large onion   1, chopped
Garlic clove   1, minced
Oil   3 tablespoons
Salt   2 teaspoons
Paprika   ¼ teaspoon
Ground cumin   1½ teaspoons
Oregano   1 tablespoon
Chili powder   3 tablespoons
Ground chili pepper   pinch
Cayenne   ⅛ teaspoon
Tomato sauce   8-ounce can
Stewed tomatoes   16-ounce can
Ground beef   1 pound
Water   5 cups

Soak beans overnight or quick-soak; drain. Cover beans with water; bring to a boil. Simmer for 2 hours, then drain. Sauté onion and garlic in oil until limp. Add next 9 ingredients and simmer 20 minutes. In a Dutch oven, brown beef; add beans, tomato mixture, and 5 cups water. Simmer 2 to 3 hours over very low heat, stirring occasionally. Serves 8 to 10.

Cheesy Chili Bean Casserole

Corn chips or broken taco shells 2 cups
Traditional Chili (see Index) 2 cups
Cheese sauce 10-ounce can
Ripe olives 2¼-ounce can, drained and chopped
Onion ¼ cup chopped
Ripe olives garnish (optional)
Avocado slices garnish (optional)

Sprinkle bottom of a 1½-quart casserole with about 2 cups corn chips.
Mix chili, cheese sauce, olives, and onion and spoon over chips. Top
with remaining chips and bake at 350° for 30 minutes. Garnish with
olives and avocado if desired. Serves 4.

Texas Baked Beans

Pinto, kidney, or navy beans 2 cups
Water 5 cups
Onion 1, thinly sliced
Oil 2 tablespoons
Unsulphured molasses ¼ cup
Salt 1½ teaspoons
Dry mustard 1 teaspoon
Chili powder 1 teaspoon

Soak beans overnight or quick-soak; drain. Bring water to a boil; slowly add
beans, reduce heat, and cover. Simmer 2 to 3 hours until beans are tender.
Sauté onion in oil until tender and add to cooked beans. Add remaining ingredients and simmer 10 to 15 minutes more. Place beans in a bean pot and
bake at 350° about 1 hour until top is browned. Serves 6 to 8.

Baked Beans with Spareribs

Pinto beans 1 pound
Water 6 cups
Beef short ribs 4 pounds
Oil 2 tablespoons
Medium onions 4, chopped
Tomato sauce 8-ounce can
Brown sugar ¼ cup
Cider vinegar 1 tablespoon
Worcestershire sauce 1 tablespoon
Prepared mustard 1 tablespoon
Salt 2 teaspoons
Chili powder 2 teaspoons
Liquid smoke 2 teaspoons or to taste (optional)
Boiling water (optional)

Put beans and water in a Dutch oven. Soak beans overnight or quick-soak. In a skillet, cook ribs in oil until well browned; remove ribs and set aside. Sauté onions in same oil until tender; stir into undrained beans. Add remaining ingredients except boiling water, and top with ribs. Cover and simmer 2½ to 4 hours until beans are tender, adding boiling water occasionally if needed. (These beans should be moist but not soupy.) Serves 4 to 6.

Deviled Baked Beans

Baked beans   4 cups or
   Canned baked beans   two 16-ounce cans
Pickle relish   1 cup
Catsup   ½ cup
Prepared horseradish   1 tablespoon
Dry mustard   1 teaspoon
Chili powder   ½ teaspoon
Worcestershire sauce   1 teaspoon
Brown sugar   ¼ cup
Butter or margarine   1 tablespoon, melted
Small corn muffins   2, crumbled

Place ½ of the beans in a greased baking dish; cover beans with relish. Combine next 6 ingredients; spoon about ⅓ of this mixture over relish and cover with remaining beans. Spread remaining sauce mixture on top of the beans. Mix butter and muffin crumbs and sprinkle thickly over top of casserole. Bake at 375° for 30 minutes, or until topping is crusty and brown. Serves 4 to 6.

Arroz con Frijoles

Rice   3 cups cooked
Refried Beans (see Index)   3 cups
Sour cream   1 cup
Gruyere cheese   3 ounces, thinly sliced
Green peppers   2, seeded and thinly sliced
Salt and pepper   to taste
Butter   2 tablespoons

Generously butter a baking dish. Spoon in a layer of rice, then a layer of beans. Add a dollop of cream, cheese slices, and pepper slices. Repeat layers until all ingredients are used. Sprinkle with salt and pepper, dot with butter, and bake at 350° about 45 minutes until heated through. Serves 6.

New Mexican Chalupas

Butter ¼ cup
Instant masa mix 1½ cups
Salt ½ teaspoon
Water about ¾ cup
Oil 2 tablespoons
Medium onion 1, chopped
Tomato sauce ½ cup
Red taco sauce 7-ounce bottle
Turkey or chicken 3 cups cooked, boned, and chopped
Refried beans (see Index) 2 cups or
    Canned refried beans 16-ounce can
Large garlic clove 1, minced
Cheddar or Monterey Jack cheese 1 cup shredded
Fresh or frozen guacamole
Sour cream garnish
Chopped chives garnish
Shredded lettuce, chopped green onions, chopped ripe olives,
    chopped fresh coriander, chopped parsley, or chopped
    tomatoes topping (optional)

Beat butter until fluffy; slowly add masa, salt, and enough water to hold dough together. Divide dough into 5 equal parts and pat each part into a 5-inch circle on waxed paper. Heat a frying pan or griddle over medium heat to 350°. Fry masa circles 3 minutes on each side; stack in oven to keep warm. Heat oil in frying pan and sauté onion until golden. Add tomato sauce and ¼ of the taco sauce; simmer uncovered until slightly thickened. Add turkey. Place in a 1½-quart casserole and set aside. Combine beans, garlic, 2 tablespoons taco sauce, and cheese. Mix well and put in a shallow pan. Heat oven to 325° and put pan in oven. Cover casserole dish and place in the oven with the bean mixture; bake 30 minutes, stirring occasionally. Spread guacamole, then bean mixture, then turkey mixture on each masa patty. Garnish with sour cream and chives; top with desired condiments. Serves 5 or 6.

Easy Chimichangas

Oil   1 tablespoon
Lean ground beef   12 ounces
Large onion   1, chopped
Large green pepper   1, seeded and chopped
Garlic clove   1, minced
Salt   ½ teaspoon
Ground cumin   ½ teaspoon
Chili powder   2 tablespoons
Cayenne   ⅛ teaspoon
Refried Beans (see Index)   ½ cup
Monterey Jack cheese   1 cup shredded
Flour tortillas   12
Oil
Sour cream   1½ cups
Frozen guacamole   two 6-ounce cans
Tomato and green chili relish

Heat oil in large skillet; add ground beef and stir to separate until lightly browned. Add onion, green pepper, and garlic and cook until onion is limp. Stir in next 5 ingredients; cook over low heat, stirring constantly, until mixture is hot. Fold in cheese. Place ¼ cup filling in center of each tortilla. Fold and roll tortilla around filling and fasten with wooden pick if needed. Fry in ¾ inch of oil at about 370° until lightly brown, turning as needed. Top with sour cream, then guacamole, then relish. Serves 6 to 8.
Note: Leftovers freeze well.

Soyburgers

Soybeans   2 cups cooked and ground
Wheat germ   1 cup
Eggs   2, beaten
Wheat germ   ½ cup
Oil   3 tablespoons

Mix soybeans, 1 cup wheat germ, and eggs; shape into 4 to 6 patties. Dip patties into remaining wheat germ and brown in oil. Serves 4 to 6.

Vegetarian Burgers

Soybeans   2 cups cooked and mashed
Brown rice   2 cups cooked (packed)
Onion   2 tablespoons chopped
Eggs   2, beaten
Salt   ½ teaspoon
Celery salt   ½ teaspoon
Green chili peppers   ¼ cup chopped (optional)

Mix all ingredients and form into 6 patties. Bake at 350° about 45 minutes until brown and serve with favorite hamburger condiments. Serves 6.

Soy–Sesame Burgers

Soybeans   1 cup
Cracked wheat   1 cup
Water
Soy sauce   2 to 3 tablespoons
Oil   3 tablespoons
Medium onion   ½, finely chopped
Sesame seeds   ⅓ cup
Whole wheat flour   ⅓ cup
Water   2 tablespoons
Whole wheat flour
Oil
Hamburger buns   4

In separate bowls, soak soybeans and cracked wheat in water over-night; drain. Grind beans in a food processor or blender. Mix with cracked wheat and next 6 ingredients; add more flour if needed to bind, and shape into patties. Dust both sides of patties with flour, then fry in a little oil until brown and crisp. Serve on hamburger buns with desired condiments. Serves 4.

Soybean Loaf

Onion ½ cup chopped
Celery 2 stalks, finely chopped
Oil 3 tablespoons
Soybeans 2 cups, cooked and pureed
Whole wheat bread crumbs 1½ cups
Tomato sauce ¾ cup
Egg 1, beaten
Sage 1 teaspoon
Honey 2 tablespoons
Salt 2 teaspoons
Garlic cloves 2, minced
Cayenne ¼ teaspoon
Tomato sauce ¼ cup

Sauté onion and celery in oil. Add remaining ingredients except ¼ cup tomato sauce. Shape into a loaf and place in a greased 9 by 5-inch loaf pan. Bake at 350° for 1 hour. Pour remaining tomato sauce over loaf and bake 5 minutes more. Serves 4 to 6.

Soybean–Millet Loaf

Soybeans 2 cups cooked and mashed
Millet 1½ cups cooked
Milk 1 cup
Safflower oil 1 tablespoon
Vegetable broth powder 1 tablespoon
Onion 2 tablespoons chopped
Salt to taste
Tomato sauce or catsup topping (optional)

Mix all ingredients except tomato sauce and press into a greased loaf pan. If desired, pour tomato sauce over loaf, or use catsup for a spicier topping. Bake at 350° for 45 minutes. Serves 4 to 5.
Variation: Add 1 or 2 beaten eggs to mixture; this will increase the already-high protein content of the loaf.

Soybean–Mushroom Loaf

Mushrooms   1 cup chopped
Celery   ½ cup chopped
Oil   2 tablespoons
Soy flour   1 tablespoon
Milk   ½ cup
Egg   1, beaten
Whole wheat bread crumbs   1 cup
Soybeans   2 cups cooked
Salt   ¼ teaspoon
Ground savory   ⅛ teaspoon

Sauté mushrooms and celery in oil; stir in flour and milk. Add remaining ingredients and mix well. Press into a greased loaf pan and bake at 350° about 45 minutes to 1 hour until brown. Serves 4 to 5.

Soy–Sunflower–Lentil Loaf

Soybeans   1 cup cooked
Sunflower seed meal   2 cups
Lentils   1 cup cooked
Parsley   2 tablespoons chopped
Milk   2 cups or
    Milk   1 cup and
    Tomato soup   1 cup
Poultry seasoning   1 teaspoon
Tomato sauce

Mix all ingredients except tomato sauce and press into a greased loaf pan. Bake at 350° for 30 to 40 minutes. Serve with tomato sauce. Serves 6.

Baked Soybeans

Soybeans   1 pound, cooked
Brown sugar   ¼ cup
Molasses   ¼ cup
Prepared mustard   1 tablespoon
Salt   1¼ teaspoons
Boiling water   about 2 cups

Combine all ingredients (there should be enough water to make a soupy mixture). Turn into a greased, deep 2-quart casserole or bean pot and bake at 300° for 5 to 7 hours or overnight. Uncover and bake 1 hour more. Serves 4.

Herb-Baked Soybeans

Soybeans   3 cups cooked
Ground marjoram   ⅛ teaspoon
Ground savory   ⅛ teaspoon
Ground rosemary   ⅛ teaspoon
Parsley   2 tablespoons chopped
Celery   1 stalk, chopped
Chives   3 tablespoons chopped
Carrots   2, finely chopped

Mix all ingredients in a casserole. Cover and bake at 350° for 45 minutes; uncover and bake 15 minutes more. Serves 4.

Baked Soybeans au Gratin

Nonfat dry milk powder   ⅓ cup
Milk   1 cup
Soybeans   1 cup cooked
Parsley   3 tablespoons chopped
Basil   ⅛ teaspoon
Carrots   2, shredded
Pimientos   2, chopped
Cheddar cheese   ½ cup shredded

Mix milk powder with milk and stir into beans. Add next 4 ingredients and turn into a casserole dish. Top with cheese and bake at 350° about 45 minutes until beans are hot and cheese is melted and golden. Serves 4.

Baked Soybeans Oriental

Soybeans   3 cups cooked, liquid drained and reserved
Ginger   1 teaspoon
Soy sauce   1 tablespoon
Apple   1, chopped
Molasses   ¼ cup
Green onions with tops   ¾ cup chopped

Combine all ingredients except bean liquid. Pour into a casserole, cover, and bake at 350° for 1 hour, adding bean liquid as needed to keep moist. Uncover and bake about 5 to 10 minutes more to brown. Serves 4.

Boston Baked Soybeans

Soybeans   1 cup, cooked, liquid reserved
Dry mustard   1 tablespoon
Onions   2, chopped
Molasses   2 to 4 tablespoons
Tomato sauce or chili sauce   to taste (optional)
Salt and pepper   to taste

Place soybeans and liquid in a bean pot or casserole. Add remaining ingredients, cover, and bake at 300° for 2 to 4 hours until beans are soft. Serves 4 to 6.

Soybean Mexicali

Soybeans   3 cups cooked
Chili powder   2 teaspoons
Onions   2, chopped
Chili peppers   2, chopped
Chili sauce   ¼ cup
Cheddar cheese   ½ cup shredded

Mix first 5 ingredients and place in a casserole. Sprinkle with cheese and bake at 350° for 1 hour. Serves 4.

Soy-Stuffed Tomatoes

Large tomatoes   6 to 8
Salt   1 teaspoon
Soybeans   3 cups cooked
Onion   1 tablespoon chopped
Green pepper   1 tablespoon chopped
Celery   ½ cup finely chopped
Wheat germ or sunflower seeds   topping
Butter

Remove pulp from center of tomatoes and lightly salt the insides; chop tomato pulp. Puree soybeans and mix with tomato pulp, onion, green pepper, and celery. Fill center of tomatoes and top with wheat germ or sunflower seeds. Dot with butter. Put tomatoes in an oiled baking pan; bake at 400° for 30 minutes, or until tomatoes are cooked and filling is thoroughly heated. Serves 6 to 8.

Soybean Creole

Soybeans   2 cups cooked
Butter   2 tablespoons
Tomatoes   16-ounce can
Fresh or frozen corn   1 cup
Green pepper   1 tablespoon chopped
Brewer's yeast   3 tablespoons (optional)
Parsley   2 tablespoons chopped
Onion   2 tablespoons chopped
Salt   ½ teaspoon
Basil   pinch

Combine all ingredients in a heavy saucepan; cover and simmer slowly over very low heat until corn is done and flavors are blended. Serves 4 to 6.

Soybean Soufflé

Eggs 3, separated
Soybeans 3 cups cooked and pureed
Onion 1 tablespoon chopped
Parsley 2 tablespoons chopped
Salt to taste

Beat egg yolks and add to soybean puree with onion, parsley, and salt. Mix thoroughly. Beat egg whites until stiff. Gently fold in the soybean mixture. Spoon into an oiled 2-quart soufflé or casserole dish. Bake at 350° about 30 minutes; serve immediately. Serves 4 to 6.

Soybean Curry

Butter or margarine ¼ cup
Curry powder 2 tablespoons
Ginger ½ teaspoon
Carrots 2½ cups thinly sliced
Large onions 2, thinly sliced
Mushrooms 8 ounces, sliced
Flour 3 tablespoons
Soybeans 1½ cups, cooked, liquid drained and 1½ cups reserved
Water chestnuts 8-ounce can
Delicious apple 1, cored and chopped
Salt and pepper to taste
Boiling water
Bean sprouts 8 ounces
Condiments*

Melt butter; stir in curry powder and ginger and cook about 1 minute. Add carrots, onions, and mushrooms and continue to cook, stirring often, until onions are limp. Stir in flour. Gradually add cooking liquid from beans; cook and stir until bubbly. Add water chestnuts and soybeans; cover and simmer about 8 minutes until carrots are tender. Stir in apple; add salt and pepper. Cover and simmer 5 minutes more. Pour boiling water oven bean sprouts and drain. Arrange them in a 2½-quart serving dish. Pour curry over sprouts and serve with condiments in small bowls. Serves 6 to 8.
* Serve curry with 3 or 4 condiments, such as plain yogurt, raisins, chutney, salted peanuts, shredded coconut, sliced bananas, chopped hard-cooked eggs, or any of your favorite condiments.

Sweet and Sour Soybeans

Soybeans   1 cup
Water
Oil   2 tablespoons
Large onion   1, cut into 1-inch squares
Large carrots   2, cut into ½-inch pieces
Garlic clove   1, minced
Green pepper   1, cut into 1-inch squares
Pineapple chunks   ¾ cup
Small tomatoes   2, cut into 1-inch cubes
Sweet and Sour Sauce
Hot rice

Soak beans in water overnight or quick-soak. Drain and reserve liquid; discard loose skins. Combine beans and liquid in a 3-quart saucepan and add enough water to cover beans. Cover and simmer 3 hours until beans are tender, adding water as needed. Drain, reserving liquid for sauce; set beans aside. In a large skillet or wok, heat oil over high heat. Add onion, carrots, and garlic. Stir-fry about 3 minutes until carrots are crisp-tender. Add green pepper and stir-fry 1 minute. Add pineapple, tomatoes, and beans. Pour Sweet and Sour Sauce over and continue cooking about 2 minutes until sauce boils and vegetables are coated. Serve over hot rice. Serves 8 to 10.

Sweet and Sour Sauce

Cornstarch   1 tablespoon
Brown sugar   ⅓ cup
Ginger   ¼ cup
Soy sauce   1 tablespoon
Wine vinegar   5 tablespoons
Reserved bean liquid or beef broth   ¼ cup

Mix cornstarch with brown sugar and ginger until smooth. Add soy sauce and vinegar and stir to make a paste. Add bean liquid and cook over medium heat, stirring constantly, about 5 to 7 minutes until sauce is transparent.

Vegetable, Bean, and Noodle Bake

Onion 1, chopped
Celery ½ head, chopped
Oil ¼ cup
Whole wheat flour 5 tablespoons
Soybeans 1 cup, cooked, liquid drained and 3 cups reserved
Carrots 2, chopped
Medium potato 1, chopped
Fresh or frozen corn 1 cup
Tomato 1, chopped
Salt 1 teaspoon
Pepper ¼ teaspoon
Dry mustard ¼ teaspoon
Sage ½ teaspoon
Basil 2 teaspoons
Whole wheat noodles 6 ounces, cooked
Tomatoes 3, sliced
Parsley ½ cup chopped
Butter (optional)

Sauté onion and celery in oil until soft. Stir in flour; continue stirring over medium heat until bubbly. Slowly add soybean liquid, stirring constantly. Reduce heat to low; add next 9 ingredients. Bring to a boil to thicken, stirring constantly; remove from heat. In a greased 9 by 13-inch baking dish, alternate layers of beans and noodles, pouring some of the vegetable sauce over each layer. Arrange tomato slices over top of casserole, sprinkle with parsley, and dot with butter. Bake at 350° for 40 minutes. Serves 6 to 8.

Herbed Soybean Casserole

Butter   3 tablespoons
Small onion   1, finely chopped
Ground thyme   ½ teaspoon
Crushed dry parsley   1 tablespoon
Garlic cloves   2, minced
Dill   ½ teaspoon
Soybeans   1 cup, cooked, liquid drained and 1 cup reserved
Medium tomatoes   2, sliced
Large crookneck squash or zucchini   2 (about 12 ounces),
   unpeeled and thinly sliced
Butter
Freshly ground pepper
Parmesan cheese   ½ cup grated

In a large pan melt butter and sauté onion until transparent, then add
next 4 ingredients. Add beans and reserved liquid and simmer about 15
minutes. Butter a large casserole; pour in ⅓ of the beans and cover with
a layer of tomatoes, then a layer of squash. Repeat layers once, then
pour remaining beans on top and dot with butter. Sprinkle with pepper
and cheese; cover and bake at 300° for 2 hours. Serves 4 to 6.

Feijao Branco Asado (Brazilian Baked Beans)

White beans   1 pound
Water
Smoked tongue or ham   1 pound
Smoked sausage   1 pound
Lean lamb   1 pound, cut into cubes
Bay leaf   1
Bacon   8 ounces, cut into cubes
Onion   ½ cup chopped
Tomatoes   1 cup peeled and chopped
Garlic clove   1, minced
Salt and pepper
Bread crumbs
Butter

Soak beans overnight or quick-soak; drain. Cover beans with water. Add smoked meats, lamb, and bay leaf, and simmer until meats are tender and beans are cooked; remove meat and set aside. Fry bacon in a Dutch oven; drain off some of the fat. Add onion and cook until onion is golden. Add tomatoes, garlic, salt, and pepper; simmer 10 minutes. Add beans, including liquid, and continue simmering 40 to 50 minutes. Adjust seasonings to taste. Pour ⅓ of the beans in a buttered casserole and place meat on top; cover with remaining beans. Sprinkle with bread crumbs and dot with butter. Bake at 375° for 30 to 40 minutes. Serves 8 to 10.

Barbecued Meat and Beans

White beans   1 pound
Water
Spicy bulk sausage   4 ounces
Bacon   4 ounces, chopped
Large barbecued chicken   1
Barbecued lamb shanks   3
Smoked pork   1 pound
Celery   1 stalk, sliced
Parsley   2 tablespoons chopped
Italian seasoning   ⅛ teaspoon
Oregano   ⅛ teaspoon
Salt   ½ teaspoon
Pepper   ¼ teaspoon
Onions   2, sliced
Garlic cloves   2, minced
Bay leaf   1
Chicken broth   1 quart
Bacon strips

Cover beans with water and soak overnight or quick-soak; simmer 1½ hours in soaking water. Fry sausage and add to beans; add bacon. Bone the chicken, lamb, and pork and add to beans. Add remaining ingredients except bacon strips and simmer 1½ hours. Remove bay leaf and discard. Line a large casserole with bacon strips. Pour in bean mixture; top with more bacon. Cover and bake at 300° for 1½ hours. Uncover and bake ½ hour more. Serves 10 to 12.

Bean Croquettes

White beans   2 cups cooked
Tomato sauce   1 cup
Onion   1 tablespoon chopped
Butter   2 tablespoons, melted
Flour   2 to 3 tablespoons
Egg yolks   2
Salt and pepper   to taste
Bread crumbs
Egg   1, beaten
Oil

Puree beans; add tomato sauce. Sauté onion in butter; stir in flour. Pour in beans and add egg yolks and salt and pepper. Cook over medium heat, stirring constantly, until mixture is thick enough to hold its shape. Cool thoroughly. Shape into croquettes: scoop out about ¼ cup at a time and mold into a fat cone. Roll in bread crumbs, then in beaten egg, then again in bread crumbs. Fry in hot oil. Serves 6 to 8.

Bean-Filled Pitas

White beans   4 cups cooked or
    Canned cannellini beans   two 16-ounce cans
Oil   5 tablespoons
Lemon juice   2 tablespoons
Oregano   1 teaspoon
Ground cumin   ½ teaspoon
Salt   ½ teaspoon
Freshly ground pepper   ¼ teaspoon
Cream cheese   3-ounce package, cubed
Medium tomatoes   2, chopped
Medium cucumber   1, peeled and diced
Pita breads   4
Parsley   2 tablespoons chopped

In a large bowl toss beans with next 6 ingredients until beans are coated. Gently fold in cheese, tomatoes, and cucumber. Cover and chill about 2 hours. Cut pita breads in half and fill each half with about ⅔ cup bean mixture, sprinkle with parsley. Serves 6 to 8.

Chili Tostadas

Corn tortillas 6
Ground beef 1 pound
Onion ½ cup chopped
Green chili peppers 3 to 5 tablespoons chopped
Salt ½ teaspoon
Chili con carne with beans 15-ounce can
Monterey Jack cheese 1 cup shredded
Lettuce ½ medium head, shredded
Large avocado 1, peeled and chopped
Medium tomatoes 3, peeled and cut into wedges
Sour cream topping (optional)
Taco sauce topping (optional)

Wrap tortillas in foil and bake at 350° for 15 minutes. Meanwhile crumble beef and cook with onion, stirring constantly, until beef is brown and onion is limp; drain fat and discard. Add peppers, salt, and chili con carne to meat mixture and stir until hot. Place tortillas on a baking sheet; spoon meat mixture evenly on tortillas. Divide cheese equally and sprinkle on meat mixture. Broil about 4 inches from heat until cheese melts. Serve immediately. In separate bowls, serve remaining ingredients as toppings. Serves 6.

Onion-and-Green-Pepper Baked Beans

Large onions 2, sliced and separated into rings
Butter 3 tablespoons
Pork and beans 2 cups or
    Canned pork and beans 16-ounce can
Tomatoes ¼ cup cooked and chopped
Catsup 2 tablespoons
Green pepper 1, seeded and sliced into rings
Brown sugar 3 tablespoons
Salt ¼ teaspoon
Pepper ¼ teaspoon
Lean bacon strips 4

Sauté onions in butter until just limp. Add remaining ingredients except bacon and turn into a 1½-quart casserole. Arrange bacon strips on top and bake uncovered at 375° for 45 minutes. Serves 4.

Breads and Desserts

Lima Bean Bread

Lima beans 1½ cups, cooked, liquid drained and 2 cups reserved
Shortening 1½ cups
Sugar 2 cups
Orange peel 1½ teaspoons grated
Unbleached flour 8 cups
Salt 1½ teaspoons
Baking soda 2 teaspoons
Cinnamon 2 teaspoons
Caraway seeds 2 tablespoons
Sunflower seeds 1½ cups hulled and salted

Puree beans with reserved liquid. Cream together shortening and sugar until very light. Add bean puree and mix well. Sift together next 5 ingredients; blend into creamed mixture (do not overmix—dry ingredients should be just moistened). Fold in caraway and sunflower seeds. Pour dough into 4 well-greased 9 by 5-inch bread pans; let stand 15 minutes. Bake at 350° for 1 hour, or until a toothpick comes out clean. Makes 4 large loaves.
Note: This bread freezes well.

Mexican Pan Bread

Onion 1, chopped
Garlic clove 1, minced
Oil 1 tablespoon
Kidney beans ½ cup, cooked and mashed, liquid drained and
    ¾ cup reserved
Egg 1, beaten
Cornmeal 1 cup
Chili powder 1 tablespoon
Ground cumin ½ teaspoon
Salt ½ teaspoon
Cheese ⅓ cup shredded

Preheat oven to 350°. Sauté onion and garlic in oil in a heavy skillet. Mix in a bowl with remaining ingredients except cheese and return to skillet. Sprinkle with cheese and bake for 10 to 12 minutes. Serves 4.

Pineapple–Garbanzo Dessert

Garbanzos 1 cup, cooked
Molasses ½ cup
Water 1 cup
Pineapple juice ½ cup
Pineapple chunks 1 cup

Remove skins from garbanzos. Mix molasses, water, and pineapple juice in a saucepan; bring to a boil. Add garbanzos and pineapple and cook until very thick. Serve cold or at room temperature in pudding bowls or glasses. Serves 6.

Fiesta Cake

Pinto beans 2 cups well cooked, liquid drained and ¼ cup reserved
Oil ½ cup
Honey ½ cup
Vanilla 1 teaspoon
Egg 1
Quick oats ½ cup
Whole wheat flour 1 cup sifted
Baking soda 1 teaspoon
Salt ½ teaspoon
Cinnamon 1 teaspoon
Ground cloves ½ teaspoon
Ground allspice ½ teaspoon
Mace ½ teaspoon
Apples 2 cups finely chopped
Raisins 1 cup
Almonds ½ cup chopped

Thoroughly mash beans in liquid. Beat together oil, honey, vanilla, and egg. Add beans and beat well. Mix together dry ingredients; add ½ the dry ingredients to bean mixture and mix slightly. Add apples, raisins, nuts, and remaining flour mixture. Stir until just mixed. Pour into a greased 8-inch square pan. Bake at 350° about 1 hour until a toothpick comes clean.

Pinto Cake

Pinto beans 2 cups cooked and mashed
Egg 1, beaten
Margarine ¼ cup, melted
Flour 1 cup
Baking soda 1 teaspoon
Salt ¼ teaspoon
Cinnamon 1 teaspoon
Ground cloves ½ teaspoon
Ground allspice ½ teaspoon
Apples 2 cups finely chopped
Raisins 1 cup
Nuts ½ cup chopped
Vanilla 2 teaspoons
Date sugar or ground nuts

Mash beans and add egg. Add margarine, mixing well. Add dry ingredients and beat thoroughly. Add apples, raisins, nuts, and vanilla; mix well. Pour into a well-greased and floured 10-inch tube pan and bake at 375° for 45 minutes. Cool and dust with date sugar or ground nuts.

U.S. and Metric Measurements

Approximate conversion formulas are given below for commonly used U.S. and metric kitchen measurements.

Teaspoons	x	5	=	milliliters
Tablespoons	x	15	=	milliliters
Fluid ounces	x	30	=	milliliters
Fluid ounces	x	0.03	=	liters
Cups	x	240	=	milliliters
Cups	x	0.24	=	liters
Pints	x	0.47	=	liters
Dry pints	x	0.55	=	liters
Quarts	x	0.95	=	liters
Dry quarts	x	1.1	=	liters
Gallons	x	3.8	=	liters
Ounces	x	28	=	grams
Ounces	x	0.028	=	kilograms
Pounds	x	454	=	grams
Pounds	x	0.45	=	kilograms
Milliliters	x	0.2	=	teaspoons
Milliliters	x	0.07	=	tablespoons
Milliliters	x	0.034	=	fluid ounces
Milliliters	x	0.004	=	cups
Liters	x	34	=	fluid ounces
Liters	x	4.2	=	cups
Liters	x	2.1	=	pints
Liters	x	1.82	=	dry pints
Liters	x	1.06	=	quarts
Liters	x	0.91	=	dry quarts
Liters	x	0.26	=	gallons
Grams	x	0.035	=	ounces
Grams	x	0.002	=	pounds
Kilograms	x	35	=	ounces
Kilograms	x	2.2	=	pounds

Temperature Equivalents

Fahrenheit	− 32	× 5	÷ 9	=	Celsius
Celsius	× 9	÷ 5	+ 32	=	Fahrenheit

U.S. Equivalents

1 teaspoon	= ⅓ tablespoon
1 tablespoon	= 3 teaspoons
2 tablespoons	= 1 fluid ounce
4 tablespoons	= ¼ cup or 2 ounces
5⅓ tablespoons	= ⅓ cup or 2⅔ ounces
8 tablespoons	= ½ cup or 4 ounces
16 tablespoons	= 1 cup or 8 ounces
⅜ cup	= ¼ cup plus 2 tablespoons
⅝ cup	= ½ cup plus 2 tablespoons
⅞ cup	= ¾ cup plus 2 tablespoons
1 cup	= ½ pint or 8 fluid ounces
2 cups	= 1 pint or 16 fluid ounces
1 liquid quart	= 2 pints or 4 cups
1 liquid gallon	= 4 quarts

Metric Equivalents

1 milliliter	= 0.001 liter
1 liter	= 1000 milliliters
1 milligram	= 0.001 gram
1 gram	= 1000 milligrams
1 kilogram	= 1000 grams

Index

Other Cookbooks from Pacific Search Press

The Apple Cookbook by Kyle D. Fulwiler
Asparagus: The Sparrowgrass Cookbook by Autumn Stanley
The Berry Cookbook by Kyle D. Fulwiler
Bone Appétit! Natural Foods for Pets by Frances Sheridan Goulart
The Carrot Cookbook by Ann Saling
The Crawfish Cookbook by Norma S. Upson
The Dogfish Cookbook by Russ Mohney
The Eggplant Cookbook by Norma S. Upson
A Fish Feast by Charlotte Wright
The Green Tomato Cookbook by Paula Simmons
Mushrooms 'n Bean Sprouts: A First Step for Would-be Vegetarians
     by Norma M. MacRae, R.D.
My Secret Cookbook by Paula Simmons
The Natural Fast Food Cookbook by Gail L. Worstman
The Natural Fruit Cookbook by Gail L. Worstman
Rhubarb Renaissance: A Cookbook by Ann Saling
Roots & Tubers: A Vegetable Cookbook by Kyle D. Fulwiler
The Salmon Cookbook by Jerry Dennon
Starchild & Holahan's Seafood Cookbook by Adam Starchild
     and James Holahan
Warm & Tasty: The Wood Heat Stove Cookbook by Margaret Byrd Adams
The Whole Grain Bake Book by Gail L. Worstman
Wild Mushroom Recipes by Puget Sound Mycological Society
The Zucchini Cookbook by Paula Simmons